MW00474024

Went
to
the
Devil

Went to the Devil

A Yankee Whaler
in the
Slave Trade

Anthony J. Connors

BRIGHT LEAF
AMHERST AND BOSTON
An imprint of University of Massachusetts Press

Copyright © 2019 by University of Massachusetts Press
All rights reserved
Printed in the United States of America

ISBN 978-1-62534-405-2 (paper); 404-5 (hardcover)

Designed by Sally Nichols
Set in Dante

Cover design by Thomas Eykemans
Cover photo by Conrad Ziebland (Wikimedia Commons).
Cover illustration from *Log of the Schooner Palmyra*,
courtesy of the New Bedford Whaling Museum.

Library of Congress Cataloging-in-Publication Data
Names: Connors, Anthony J., author.
Title: Went to the devil : a Yankee whaler in the slave trade / Anthony J.
  Connors.
Description: Amherst : Bright Leaf, an imprint of University of Massachusetts
  Press, [2019] | Includes bibliographical references and index.
Identifiers: LCCN 2018051740 | ISBN 9781625344045 (hardcover) | ISBN
  9781625344052 (pbk.) | ISBN 9781613766521 (ebook) | ISBN 9781613766538
  (ebook)
Subjects: LCSH: Davoll, Edward S. | Davoll, Edward S.—Ethics. | Slave
  traders—Massachusetts—New Bedford—Biography. | Whaling
  masters—Massachusetts—New Bedford—Biography. | Slave trade—Moral and
  ethical aspects—History—19th century. | Slave trade—Cuba—History—19th
  century. | Slave trade—Africa—History—19th century. |
  Whaling—Massachusetts—New Bedford—History—19th century. | Seafaring
  life—History—19th century. | New Bedford (Mass. —Biography.
Classification: LCC F74.N5 C66 2019 | DDC 381/.44092 [B] —dc23 LC record
  available at https://lccn.loc.gov/2018051740

British Library Cataloguing-in-Publication Data
A catalog record for this book is available
from the British Library.

For Sharon

CONTENTS

A NOTE ON THE TRANSATLANTIC SLAVE TRADE

The Buckeye did not bring palm oil or ivory, except
the ivory teeth of her living cargo.

—*New York Times,* January 17, 1861

The transatlantic slave trade was the forced migration of
more than twelve million Africans to the Americas between
1501 and 1867. Slavery has of course existed since antiquity: the
Mesopotamians, Egyptians, Chinese, Greeks, Romans, and
many other cultures all had slaves. Some were captives of war,
but increasingly slaves came from afar, transported through
a complex exchange system that we call the slave trade. Our
story is concerned with a particular (and probably best-known)
system, the African or transatlantic slave trade: the purchase of
men, women, and children in western Africa for transportation
to slave markets in Brazil, the Caribbean, and North America.
This began with Columbus and proved so lucrative that the
Portuguese, Dutch, British, and others greedily took up the
trade. New World slavery became race based and hereditary,
condemning people of color to ownership by others, violent
discrimination and abuses of human rights, and the horror of
passing on the same degraded status to their children.[1]

Plantation slavery has often been considered primitive and
inefficient, unable to stand up to the rigors of modern international capitalism. On the contrary, the slave trade that emerged

in the nineteenth century was very modern, with capital, ships, agents, and nodes of operation in New York, Europe, the Caribbean, Brazil, and Africa, along with many accomplices— sailors, middlemen, customs officials, lawyers—who were only too willing to participate. As slave trade historians David Eltis and David Richardson point out, "The transatlantic slave trade was perhaps the most thoroughly multinational business of the early modern era." Karl Marx recognized that Africa had been turned into "a warren for the commercial hunting of black-skins [that] signalized the rosy dawn of the era of capitalist production." Rather than slowly fading away in the face of more innovative economic systems, this nineteenth-century slavery system saw an expansion of the slave trade, with Africans treated as products just like other goods that had been commodified through mercantilism, industrial capital-ism, and advances in transportation.[2] To slave traders, Africans were "black gold."

While the practice of slavery persisted, the trade in slaves came under fire for the particular brutality and mortality of the Middle Passage across the Atlantic Ocean, during which about one out of seven slaves perished.[3] Engaging in the African slave trade was prohibited by both Massachusetts (1788) and federal law (1794). The federal act of 1794 made it illegal to build or fit out a vessel in the United States for slaving, and an amendment in 1800 made it illegal for any American citizen to take part in a slaving voyage. An act of Congress in 1807 (effective January 1, 1808) prohibited the importation into the United States or its territories of "any negro, mulatto, or person of color" to be held as slaves. Penalties were severe, with fines up to $10,000 and jail terms of five to ten years. An amendment in 1819 au-thorized the president to send armed vessels to cruise the coast of Africa to thwart slave traders, which led to the creation of the U.S. Navy's African Squadron. A further refinement in 1820 stipulated that slave trading was piracy and therefore punish-able by death.[4]

None of these prohibitions did much to suppress the slave trade, which continued and even accelerated in the 1850s as Cuba's sugar production increased dramatically (not incidentally, the United States was the biggest market for Cuban sugar).[5] The laws were ineffective because of poor enforcement, sham vessel ownership, forged papers, and general indifference to a tragedy that was taking place somewhere else, far away. The agents of the slave trade were organized, well financed, and unscrupulous; they had access to clever lawyers and were generous in their bribes and ruthless with witnesses and juries. Various administrations of U.S. presidents were generally indifferent; in fact, in ten of the fifteen terms between 1800 and 1860, the president was a slaveholder.

The world had an insatiable appetite for sugar, coffee, tobacco, and cotton, all products that were grown on plantations by gangs of brutally controlled slaves. The modernized Atlantic slave trade of the nineteenth century ensured that there was a steady supply of Africans to work the plantations of the New World. More slaves were transported to Brazil (44 percent) than to any other country or colony; by contrast, only about 4 percent went to North America. When the Brazil trade ended in 1850, due mainly to suppression by the British navy, Cuba emerged as the primary destination and the involvement of Americans increased sharply. As W. E. B. Du Bois put it in his pioneering study, "The American slave-trade finally came to be carried principally by United States capital, in United States ships, officered by United States citizens, and under the United States flag."[6] By the 1850s the transatlantic slave trade had become a highly efficient and extraordinarily profitable web of money, ships, and agents that drew men like Captain Edward Davoll, the main subject of this book, into the appalling business of buying and selling human beings.

ACKNOWLEDGMENTS

Any work of history owes a debt to previous historians, some known, some lost over time. This book is rooted in local history, and I have been fortunate to find gems that provide depth and context to the story. I have also relied on contemporary historians, and a wonderful array of friends, and my only fear is that I have forgotten to publicly thank some of them. With that in mind, I would like to express my gratitude to the many who helped.

The late Richard C. Kugler, former director of the New Bedford Whaling Museum, was the first person to bring to my attention Captain Edward Davoll, who became the focus of this biography. The whaling museum continued to be my richest source for the book—in documents, images, and advice. I particularly thank Senior Historian Michael P. Dyer, who possesses an astonishing knowledge of whaling. Whenever I had a question, Mike was ready with answers or further sources, and he saved me from numerous mistakes. Mark Procknik was also generous with his time and expertise, especially regarding the book illustrations. Bow Van Riper of the Martha's Vineyard Museum was also very helpful with images. Richard Donnelly generously shared a private trove of photos and letters of the Davoll family.

The other organization that played a vital role in the development of this project is the Westport (MA) Historical Society, under the exceptional leadership of Executive Director Jenny O'Neill. Jenny and I had many talks on the subject, and she sat through endless iterations of my presentations. Her insights and unflagging enthusiasm were invaluable. Also contributing from the historical society were Lenora Robinson, who discovered an intriguing 1920s newspaper article that bore oddly on the 1860 voyage of the slaver *Brutus*, and Kathleen McAreavey, who brought to my attention the opportunity to present an early, condensed version of this project at the Dublin Seminar at Historic Deerfield in 2016. This proved to be an important step on the road toward book-length treatment. My thanks to Director Peter Benes and the seminar participants.

I greatly appreciate the feedback and helpful conversations and encouragement from knowledgeable friends and colleagues, including my brother Ned Connors, Betty Slade, David Cole, Al Lees, Richard Gifford, Davison Paull, Skip Carter, Judy Lund, Len Travers (University of Massachusetts Dartmouth), Drew R. McCoy (Clark University), Lee Blake (New Bedford Historical Society), Cliff McCarthy (Belchertown Historical Association), and Karla Ingemann (Bermuda Archives).

The staff at the National Archives in Waltham, Massachusetts, provided access to valuable trial records. Jared Johnson and my brother Tom helped with National Archives research in Washington, DC. The Special Collections staff at the New Bedford Public Library aided my access to nineteenth-century newspapers. Aaron Usher and Ned Connors restored digital images from otherwise unusable daguerreotypes.

I can't say enough about the people of the University of Massachusetts Press. Matt Becker, the executive editor, took an early and enthusiastic interest in the project and moved it along expertly. At every stage my contacts were professional and collegial, making me feel like part of the team (even the task of indexing was—sort of—fun). I would like to especially thank Courtney Andree (marketing manager), Rachael DeShano (production editor), Sally Nichols (editorial, design, and production manager), and Annette Wenda (copyeditor), as well as

Thomas Eykemans, who created the appropriately foreboding cover design.

Matt also chose excellent anonymous readers for the peer review. Not only were they very knowledgeable about both whaling and the slave trade and incisive in their comments, but they went out of their way to help me succeed, and the book is much improved factually and organizationally for their suggestions.

Finally, I'm especially thankful for Sharon—my wife, best friend, and great proofreader who with love, and stamina, read every word, many times.

Went
to
the
Devil

INTRODUCTION

ON THE LAM IN BERMUDA

In November 1861, Captain Edward Davoll prepared the whaling schooner *Palmyra* to winter over at Bermuda. He wrote to his wife that he would be home as soon as this task was completed, yet he lingered in Bermuda for six months. Winter storms were a danger, and, in this opening year of the Civil War, he had been told of Confederate pirates in the vicinity. These excuses masked his real reason for delay. A year earlier he had outfitted the ship *Brutus* for a whaling cruise and guided it from New Bedford, Massachusetts, to the Azores. Then, with the captain remaining behind, the ship went on under the command of the first mate to the Congo River, where they purchased more than five hundred slaves and transported them to Cuba for sale. Davoll had played a crucial part in the slaving voyage—fitting out the *Brutus* to look like a legitimate whaler to deceive the port authorities and the federal revenue cutter patrolling outside New Bedford Harbor. His role completed, Davoll had returned home and quickly secured a legitimate whaling command on the *Palmyra*. The longer he stayed out, the better the chances that the rumors of illegal slaving that had swirled around New Bedford would die down. But as he cruised the whaling grounds between the Azores and Bermuda, he received news that the *Brutus*'s slaving operation had been discovered—thanks to a crew member who told federal prosecutors of the sham whaling, the purchase of slaves, the suffocating Atlantic crossing and scores of deaths at sea, and the sale of the survivors to a Cuban sugar plantation. The owners of the false whaler had been arrested, and Davoll feared that he would face indictment and prison. Finally, though, after months of wavering in Bermuda, he decided to return to his wife and daughter in New Bedford. He could not have been surprised when a federal marshal knocked at his door.

Davoll was from the nearby town of Westport, where he had learned the whaling trade at seventeen, later moving to New Bedford for voyages with increasing responsibility. Whaling was a respectable career for a mariner along the south coast of Massachusetts. It could also be lucrative: the main road leading to the Westport wharves was lined with graceful Greek Revival homes of whaling captains, agents, and investors—an indication of their wealth and status in town. There was no reason, if he applied himself, he couldn't have one of those homes as well. This smart and ambitious young man did apply himself, and by the age of twenty-five he had attained the rank of captain. He built a reputation as a respected—if not always liked—whaling master in an industry that appeared to be thriving. But by the late 1850s his prospects had diminished, due to changes in the industry but also to his own bad luck, leading him to a series of fateful decisions that would ruin him and his family. In recounting Davoll's life, we discover not only how he got to this juncture but also why a devoted family man, just thirty-eight years old, with nine whaling voyages to his credit, would risk his career and his freedom to engage in the loathsome and illegal slave trade.

On one level this is an account of the rise and downfall of one individual, a man who had shown tremendous promise in a prosperous industry but found himself trapped in a job that separated him from his family for increasingly longer periods of time and unable to escape the loneliness, drudgery, and dangers of his trade. This is also the story of the resurgence of the Atlantic slave trade in the decade before the Civil War, as Cuba produced an ever-greater percentage of the world's sugar, a commodity entirely reliant on plantation slavery. This revival of the slave trade coincided with the realization within the whaling community—particularly in its preeminent port, New Bedford—that its most profitable days were over, an awareness that drove some men to desperate measures. What developed was a peculiar relationship between whaling and the slave trade, made possible by the dimming prospects for whaling and the crafty New York slaving agents and their worldwide network of financiers who were able to exploit whalers' economic uncertainty and moral indifference to their advantage.

This moral apathy does not match New Bedford's reputation as a bastion of antislavery sentiment. The Quaker-influenced city had provided sanctuary to the runaway slave Frederick Douglass and was an important stop on the Underground Railroad. Yet New Bedford was not immune to the expansion of New York–based slaving to coastal New England towns. How deep was New Bedford's commitment to abolitionism? Who knew about the whaling industry's complicity in slaving, and who did anything about it? Davoll's life, as he slid from respectable whaler to accomplice in slave-trading voyages, provides a glimpse into social and economic issues that allowed a surprising number of people—captains, ordinary sailors, agents, outfitters, and government officials—to conspire in this appalling business.

While the story begins in the relatively sleepy whaling port of Westport and moves to the bustling wharves of New Bedford, this isn't just a New England tale. It takes us to the Azores and the North Atlantic, to the Indian Ocean and Australia, and finally—tragically—to the slave-trading coast of Africa and the sugar plantations of Cuba. It's a story of the often romantically depicted but ultimately brutal business of whaling and of shipboard disease, fears of "native" attack, violent storms and shipwreck, the toll of long separation from family, the cruel punishment of seamen, and the moral drift from legitimate work toward engagement in the slave trade. Edward Davoll's life conveys the rigors of a seafaring life at a critical time in the history of whaling and shows how the lure of easy money could tempt a man of good reputation and seemingly high moral character to engage in the flourishing Africa-to-Cuba slave trade.

These events take place at a critical time in American history. The tumultuous 1850s brought increasingly radical antislavery activism, the financial panic of 1857, and escalating polarization over whether a nation half slave and half free could survive. As Captain Davoll's personal drama unfolds, the country is plunging toward civil war.

CHAPTER 1

A WHALING CAREER

O ur story begins in the rural maritime town of Westport, Massachusetts, where Edward S. Davoll was born on September 21, 1822. Westport was a young town then, having separated from Dartmouth only thirty-five years previously. But two of the Dartmouth villages that became part of Westport were well developed by 1700. One was a peninsula at the confluence of the Acoaxet and Noquochoke Rivers,[1] called Peckacheque Point (later renamed Westport Point), where the maritime docks were situated just inside the entrance to a sheltered harbor leading to the Atlantic Ocean. The wharves at the Point would be an important place in Edward's early career as a whaleman. The other village was an industrial and commercial settlement known as the Head of Westport River, or simply "the Head." That's where the Davoll family lived, a mile or so south of the town landing where whaling and merchant ships were built.

Edward was the first of five children of Jeremiah and Barbara (Allen) Davoll, who made a respectable living growing corn and oats and raising sheep on their sixty acres of farmland.[2] The younger children were George (born 1826), Mary (1828), and William (1830). A daughter, Hannah, was born in 1835, but died two years later. We have little personal information about the family except for Edward's cousin Ruby Devol Finch (1804–66).

A painter relatively unknown outside of Westport, Ruby Devol (later Finch) is now considered "one of the most uniquely creative female American folk artists of her time." She recorded the major events in the lives of friends and neighbors in vividly drawn watercolor paintings. Unrecognized in her lifetime, her paintings are now valuable, not only for their artistic merit but as documentation of the clothing, social customs, furniture, and architecture of Westport in the early nineteenth century.[3]

The Davoll family had deep roots in southeastern Massachusetts, and as Ruby Devol's name indicates, there were various spellings of the family name: Devol, Devoll, Davol, Davoll, DeVol. Even official documents often misspelled Edward's name.

Little is known about Edward's schooling. There were nineteen school districts across this geographically large rural town, and the school at the Head was within easy walking distance of the Davoll home. Westport's schools had once offered a classical education, including Greek and Latin, but by the time Edward started the town had switched to a more practical curriculum better suited to the kinds of work available in this agricultural and maritime area and emphasized basic writing and math skills.[4]

We don't know how many years Edward attended school. There was no high school in town until 1868, so his education probably ended after eighth grade. We can, however, infer something about the quality of his education. Edward's letters indicate a very good grasp of grammar, a solid vocabulary, and reasonably correct and consistent spelling. He also had the math skills to become an expert navigator. If the purpose of his schooling was to train him for the profession of master mariner, it was a success.

There is no record of what Edward did between the time he finished school and began his maritime career. As the eldest son of a farmer, he probably helped out on the family farm, but it is also likely that he gained some experience on the water, living close by the river and, as most local boys did, spending time in boats. Perhaps he ventured downstream to the Point, and even a bit farther, to the harbor mouth and the Atlantic Ocean.

At seventeen it was time to get a job that could lead to a career, and there were many choices for an intelligent young man in Westport in 1840. If farming didn't interest him, there was fishing, one of the dominant businesses in town. There was shipbuilding at the Town Landing, and there were several gristmills and a sawmill along the streams just north of the Head. If he wanted factory work, Fall River was just ten miles to the northwest: there were jobs available at the many cotton mills or the Fall River Iron Works. About the same distance to the east was New Bedford—later to become an industrial giant, but in 1840 doing well in fishing and maritime trade along the Eastern Seaboard or with the West Indies. More important, by 1840 New Bedford was just overtaking Nantucket as the nation's whaling capital. It was a fast-growing town that in a few years would become a city—the richest per capita in America.

Whaling was the third-largest industry in Massachusetts at this time, behind only cotton textiles and shoes. Whales were sought for their oil and their "bone." This whalebone was actually baleen, the long, flexible strips of keratin that hang from the mouths of many whales (notably not toothed varieties such as the sperm whale) and are used to strain their food supply (krill) from the ocean. Because of its strength and flexibility, baleen was useful in the manufacture of products like corset stays, buggy whips, skirt hoops, and umbrella ribs—a nineteenth-century plastic. Ordinary whale oil came from the blubber of a variety of whales, such as right whales, bowheads, and humpbacks. This was not the most prized oil but had commercial value for lighting and industrial lubrication. If better whales could not be taken, as the saying went, "brown oil is better than no oil."[5]

Well known to us thanks to Melville's *Moby-Dick,* the sperm whale could reach sixty feet in length and weigh sixty tons. Sperm whale oil had superior lubricating qualities, and when used in oil lamps it burned brightly and without odor. It sold for about double the price of oil from other whales. Even more valuable was spermaceti, the waxy substance in their heads (called "head matter"), which produced bright, clean-burning, odorless—and expensive—candles. The sperm whale was the primary target of New England whalers.

If New Bedford was the leviathan of the whaling industry, Westport was a small fish. Yet judged by number of whaling voyages, Westport ranked eighth in the United States, a respectable showing for a small port.[6] The town's first connection with whaling was industrial, based on the sawmills, iron forge, and bog iron deposits just north of the Head of Westport, where local men built ships and forged iron products for the New Bedford whaling business. But with the harbor at Westport Point opening to the Atlantic, the town developed a whaling industry of its own. The first recorded Westport whaling voyage was in 1775, but the American Revolution delayed further cruises. There were a few in the 1790s, but it was not until 1803 that whaling took off. Despite its tricky harbor entrance, narrow and shallow channel, and tight wharf area, Westport Point was an active whaling port until 1879—a span of more than seventy-five years.

While Westport was part of the New Bedford Customs District, it had its local owners, agents, captains, shipyards, outfitting store, sailmakers, coopers—everything (except insurance companies) to manage, equip, and conduct whaling voyages. The agents directed the voyages and were usually part-owners. The major Westport agents all had impressive homes, most in the latest Greek Revival style, along Main Road, near the town docks. Andrew Hicks was on a level with many New Bedford agents: he built eight vessels and had an interest in eleven ships that made a total of seventy-eight voyages.

Alexander Cory and Gideon Davis owned the chandlery (the maritime supply store) close to the docks. There were also several cooper shops nearby that provided the large number of barrels and casks required for fresh water and whale oil. With all these resources, Westport was a self-sustaining whaling port, and it was from this harbor that young Davoll began his career as a whaleman.

Edward Davoll went to sea for the first time in 1840, at the age of seventeen, on the brig *Elizabeth* of Westport Point. He was described as five feet eight with light skin and brown hair. An indication that he might have had some previous maritime experience is his listing as an ordinary seaman rather than a "greenhand." His portion of the proceeds, or "lay," is another indication: one-sixtieth, quite high for a first voyage. The crew consisted of the captain, two officers (mates), and twelve men, and in one respect it was unusual: the captain was Pardon Cook, one of the few black whaling captains, and the crew of the *Elizabeth* was a "checkerboard" mix of black and white mariners. The two mates, Asa and Rodney Wainer, were of black and Indian heritage. Given Edward Davoll's later activities, it is tempting to speculate on the effect of this first voyage under a black captain and officers, but there is simply no evidence to go on.[7]

A brig was a sailing vessel with two masts, both square rigged. The *Elizabeth* was rather small for a whaler: at 130 tons, it was the smallest of the seven whaling vessels that sailed out of Westport that year (the average was 171 tons, compared to more than 300 tons for New Bedford whalers).[8] A whaling vessel was a sailor's cramped rat- and cockroach-infested home for months to years. The worst quarters were in the forecastle, in the forward part of the ship, "before the mast." This is where the ordinary seamen and greenhands slept. As one whaleman described it, "The forecastle was black and slimy with filth, very small and hot as an oven. It was filled with a compound of foul air, smoke, sea-chests, soap-kegs, greasy pans, tainted meat, Portuguese ruffians, and sea-sick Americans."[9] Whether the *Elizabeth* fit this description or not, it certainly was unpleasant.

The most disagreeable duties fell to the foremast hands, especially those who had no experience. As Richard Henry Dana Jr. remarked in *Two Years before the Mast,* "There is not so helpless and pitiable object in the world as a landsman beginning a sailor's life."[10] The foremast men climbed the rigging and handled the sails as the mate ordered and stood watches (usually four hours). From the masthead they scanned the ocean for whales and sang out when they spotted one. In *Moby-Dick,* Herman Melville describes the precarious post high above the deck: "Your most usual point of perch is the head of the t' gallant-mast, where you stand upon two thin parallel sticks (almost peculiar to whalemen) called the t' gallant crosstrees. Here, tossed about by the sea, the beginner feels about as cosy as he would standing on a bull's horns." To Ishmael this is a place for contemplation of nature, but, he warns, "move your foot or hand an inch; slip your hold at all; and your identity comes back in horror. Over Descartian vortices you hover. And perhaps, at midday, in the fairest weather, with one half-throttled shriek you drop through that transparent air into the summer sea, no more to rise for ever. Heed it well, ye Pantheists!"[11]

Just as terrifying was the job of manning the whaleboat, rowing miles from the ship to get uncomfortably close to creatures twice the length of the whaleboat. Once captured and brought back to the ship, the whale was processed by stripping off the blubber, cutting it into pieces, and boiling it in the tryworks to render it into oil. There were also long, boring stretches when no whales were seen. A captain usually kept the men busy at all times, to maintain discipline. If the crew was lucky, Sunday was a day off. A whaleship has been described as a military unit, a hospital, a prison, an insane asylum, an industrial enterprise, a family—all under the unconditional control of a potentially tyrannical leader. It was at times all of these.[12]

Davoll's first voyage was what was known as a "plum-pudding" cruise—a short trip that would typically cross the Atlantic Ocean to the Azores, then south to the Cape Verde Islands, back across the ocean to the Brazil Banks, up through the West Indies, and back home in six months or so.[13] And this 1840 voyage of the *Elizabeth* was typical: out from June 24 to November 1 (just over four months), in the Atlantic. Two weeks out, Davoll encountered his first whale, but they were unable to capture it. It was a full two months before a whale was successfully brought in, a large sperm whale that yielded 90 barrels of oil.[14] They returned with 150 barrels of sperm oil, about one-third less than the previous voyage of the *Elizabeth*. While probably not a losing voyage, it is unlikely that the owners made much of a profit, nor would there have been much for the crew to share. The first-time whaleman probably earned no more than thirty dollars.[15]

Six months after returning from his first whaling voyage, young Davoll signed up for another. He must have been employed during his time at home (having earned little on the *Elizabeth*) but chose to continue as a whaleman. Again he would sail out of Westport Point, but on a different vessel, the *Mexico,* commanded by Gideon H. Smith, a veteran of three voyages as master. Davoll's shipping papers specified that no "distilled spirituous liquors" could be brought on board. Also prohibited was "the introduction of any woman or women into the ship for licentious purposes." Sailors who disobeyed these rules would forfeit their entire share in the voyage. Curiously, Davoll signed on as a greenhand, a lower rank—and lower lay—than on his previous voyage. His one-ninetieth lay was, in fact, the lowest of the entire crew except for the steward.[16]

The *Mexico* was a 137-ton brig with a deck length of seventy feet, built in 1826 in Newport, Rhode Island, just a bit over ten miles by water from Westport Point. Only slightly bigger than the *Elizabeth,* it was used for Atlantic cruises, sometimes as far as the Cape Verde Islands off the coast of Africa. It was seaworthy—"tight in her bottom," the captain said—but the forecastle (or fo'c'sle) leaked badly all during the voyage due to poor caulking of the deck. Unfortunately for Davoll and the other seamen, the dark, soggy fo'c'sle was their home.

The records don't indicate much about the first part of the voyage, which began August 31, 1842. Sometime in early winter they reached the coast of Africa, where Davoll experienced his first death at sea when crew member Antonin Cooper "departed this life of malignant fever."[17] Edward saw other drawbacks of whaling life as well. When they stopped at the island of Dominica for fresh fruit, a crew member deserted. They also had a problem with the cook—"the worst dispositioned man . . . I ever sailed with," in the captain's opinion—who had been confined in irons.

By February 1 they were at Puerto Rico, with only 30 barrels of sperm oil. "It has been 5 mo 7 d[ays] since we have seen the spout of a sp[erm] whale," the captain lamented, "and the Lord only nows [*sic*] when we shall again." A month later they reached Grand Cayman, with no additional oil. But whaling improved in the Gulf of Mexico: the captain reported 200 barrels at the end of May. The ship returned to Westport just before the Fourth of July with 236 barrels of sperm oil. For a voyage of ten months, it was a disappointing haul. (The *Mexico* had usually brought in more than 300 barrels and three times had returned with over 400 barrels.) Worse, the price of sperm oil had dropped from $1 a gallon to 63 cents. The owners, Davis & Cory, who ran the provisioning store at the Westport Point wharves, might have made a small profit, but it is unlikely that Edward was satisfied with his share. The 236 barrels (7,434 gallons) of sperm oil, at 63 cents per gallon, would be worth about $4,700 and the crew's share about $1,600. Davoll's one-ninetieth lay would earn about $17. This was no way to make a living.[18]

Now twenty-one, Davoll apparently enjoyed whaling well enough and was sufficiently adept at it to make it his career. It was a highly regarded profession, despite the grimness of the actual work. Perhaps he saw himself in the almost heroic terms that the noted Westport artist and writer Clifford Ashley, reflecting on his own experience on a whaler, depicted the New England whaleman:

> Whaling was a life that required certain high qualifications. It may be taken for granted that the men who were attracted to it were beyond the average in physical courage, or they would not have planned to face in frequent combat the greatest animal that ever lived; and that they were beyond the average in resolution and ambition, since they were willing to renounce, for years on end the food, the comforts, and the amusements of shore, and the companionship and society of friends, wives, and children; and to endure hardships and labor unremittingly, often against overwhelming misfortune, until the purpose of their voyage was accomplished.[19]

But Davoll's career would not advance in Westport. The town was now home port to 11 whalers, all of them smaller than average and most suitable only for Atlantic cruises. At this time, New Bedford had 254 whaling vessels, far outpacing Nantucket (75); New London, Connecticut (70); and Sag Harbor, Long Island (62).[20] So, for an ambitious young man with two voyages under his belt, the logical place to move was to New Bedford. A large town on the verge of becoming a city, New Bedford had a population of more than twelve thousand, four times that of Westport. There were seven thousand people employed in jobs related to whaling in New Bedford. He would be one young man among many, but he had talent, experience, and ambition. He also had some education, and

FIGURE I. This painting of the New Bedford waterfront, ca. 1848, is part of the *Grand Panorama of a Whaling Voyage 'Round the World,* by Benjamin Russell and Caleb Purrington. Courtesy of the New Bedford Whaling Museum.

he was white—a not insignificant social and economic advantage. New Bedford was less than ten miles from his home, with plenty of stores, bars, and entertainment, so Davoll might have already been familiar with it.[21]

The purported beauty of the town was real. According to Herman Melville, "Nowhere in all America will you find more patrician-like houses; parks and gardens more opulent, than in New Bedford." But, he added, "In New Bedford, actual cannibals stand chatting at street corners; savages outright; many of whom yet carry on their bones unholy flesh. It makes a stranger stare." While this is his fictionalized view of the city in *Moby-Dick,* other visitors agreed on the mix of the beautiful and the exotic. There was also a dark side, inhabited by sailors and those catering to their various needs. One observer described a scene of whalemen recently discharged from their ship—"a motley and savage looking crew, unkempt and unshaven, capped with the head-gear of various foreign climes and people—under the friendly guidance of a land shark, hastening to the sign of the *Mermaid,* the *Whale,* or the *Grampus,* where, in drunkenness and debauchery, they may soonest get rid of their hard-earned wages, and in the shortest space of time arrive at that condition of poverty and disgust of shore life that must induce them to ship for another four years cruise."[22] Young Davoll would have to find his way through a maze of hazards as he pursued better opportunities in the burgeoning whaling industry.

He soon found his ship, the bark *Cornelia,* built in Westport in 1832. At 216 tons, it was considerably larger than his two previous whalers, plus, as a bark, it had three masts—a much more impressive vessel. The captain was Daniel Flanders, who had made eight prior voyages as master. This would be Edward's first experience whaling in the Indian Ocean. He had made a significant improvement in his status: he was now a boatsteerer, an important role that included wielding the harpoon on one of the whaleboats. (After the harpooner struck a whale, it was the mate who killed it, and at this point the harpooner became the steerer of the whale boat—hence the confusing term *boatsteerer.*)[23] Boatsteerers ranked above ordinary seamen but still below the mates (officers); their privileges included taking their meals in the main cabin, after the captain and mates had eaten, and sleeping in the steerage midway between the officers' cabins and the forecastle. These were not luxury quarters but a decided improvement for Davoll.

The *Cornelia* left New Bedford on December 12, 1843. They probably whaled in the Azores before heading to the South Atlantic and by May 1844 were in the vicinity of the remote island of St. Helena, reporting only 30 barrels of sperm whale oil. This was his first time below the equator, and he would have been subjected to an initiation ceremony—usually involving a visit from "Old Neptune" and (except on temperance ships) a lot of alcohol.[24] To the blindfolded victims, who might be tarred or shaved with a piece of iron hoop, it was physical and mental hazing but amusing to the salts who had already been through it. Once the ordeal was over, Davoll could chalk up another milestone in his whaling career.[25]

For eight months there was no update on their location in the *Whalemen's Shipping List*, the industry's weekly newspaper, an indication they were encountering few homeward-bound ships to relay their current status (and to let worried relatives know that, at last report, all was well). The next information was from Tristan da Cunha, another remote British-controlled volcanic island fifteen hundred miles south of St. Helena. Tristan was often used by whalers as a stopping place for fresh vegetables and water. They now had 150 barrels of sperm oil and 150 barrels of whale oil in the hold.[26]

From there Captain Flanders guided the *Cornelia* around the Cape of Good Hope and into the Indian Ocean. From April to September they cruised in the vicinity of Johanna Island, north of Madagascar. This was exotic territory for a first-time visitor, and it is likely that the crew got a taste of local color when the ship stopped at Johanna. The whaling was good too, and with 600 barrels of sperm oil, the bark headed back into the Atlantic Ocean. At St. Thomas, then under Danish control, the captain reported that they would cruise for six to eight months more, but, perhaps due to orders from the agent, they were back home in six weeks.

On April 27, 1845, the *Cornelia* docked at New Bedford. It had been away two years and four months. In the hold were 625 barrels of sperm oil, 390 barrels of whale oil, and 2,800 pounds of whalebone. At current prices the total value of the catch was $22,306. We don't know Davoll's lay on this voyage, but a typical share of the total catch for a boatsteerer would have earned him about $250. It might be hard to imagine this as an adequate reward for more than two years' work, but it was an improvement over his Westport voyages. The captain of the *Cornelia* probably made $1,400 and the first mate $900, which only encouraged Davoll to aim higher on his next cruise.[27]

The next time came soon. In less than two months he was aboard the *Cornelia* again. There is no record of his rank on this voyage, but given what we know about his rapid rise through the ranks, he must have signed on as a mate. The mates—typically first, second, and third—were officers who carried out the captain's orders and interacted directly with the crew. Each mate was also in charge of one of the whaleboats (the captain often commanded a whaleboat as well). His role, as described earlier, was to steer the boat as it approached the whale, and after the harpooner struck the whale, the mate would switch places with the harpooner and deliver the killing blow with his lance. A typical lay for a mate was between one-twenty-fifth and one-fiftieth, a big step up from boatsteerer. Other benefits included eating at the captain's table, with more meat and fresh vegetables than the rest of the crew, and small cabins for sleeping.

On June 23, 1846, the *Cornelia* left the port of New Bedford, bound again for the Indian Ocean. The first stop was Fayal (Faial), in the Azores, where on August 3 they reported 100 barrels of sperm whale oil.[28] It was a full year before their specific location was again listed in the whaling newspaper—at Johanna, near Mozambique, with 330 barrels of sperm oil. In November 1847 they were cruising in the vicinity of Europa, an uninhabited island in the channel between Madagascar and the mainland of Mozambique. Five months later they were back at St. Helena, in the South Atlantic, heading home, with 500 barrels of sperm oil in the hold. It took another three months of cruising to make their way back to New Bedford, arriving July 31, 1848, with 630 barrels of sperm oil and 70 barrels of lower-grade whale oil. They also carried 4,600 pounds of whalebone, but 4,000 of that belonged to the bark *Cadmus* of Sag Harbor, Long Island. As often happened when homeward-bound whalers encountered outward-bound vessels, Captain Flanders had agreed to transport some of their catch to market, for which the *Cornelia* owners would collect a transportation fee.[29]

Out two years and one month, the *Cornelia*'s oil was worth a bit over $20,000. (Sperm oil now fetched $1 a gallon, ordinary whale oil only 33 cents.) It isn't clear if Davoll had shipped as first, second, or third mate on this voyage, but assuming second mate his share would have been about $500. This was double what he made on the previous voyage as boatsteerer (and for a shorter voyage). Moving up in rank in the whaling industry was paying off.

What he was doing with his increased earnings was another matter. According to his youngest brother, William, Edward "spent nearly all of his voyage before he sailed." This suggests that Edward was racking up debts that he would pay off from future earnings. The comment was in reference to their brother, George, who had followed Edward into the whaling trade and had apparently taken up his spending habits. William was eight years younger than Edward (four younger than George) and expressed this opinion, among others, in a revealing letter to Edward during the *Cornelia's* 1846–48 cruise. George had returned from a whaling voyage and after running around for a while decided to go back to school at the Head of Westport, but after six weeks "swore that he would go no more for he had got learning enough." William, with a nice touch of sarcasm at seventeen, admitted that unlike George, he did not have learning enough and would continue his education. (William did not follow his brothers into whaling and became a jeweler.)

But the real subject of William's letter is Edward's love life. Away for long stretches of time, whalemen had difficulty holding on to sweethearts. William warns that "Eli P. Lawton waited on your June meeting gal. Look out or you will lose her sure as hell." Whoever that may be, William is more concerned about a girl named Sallee Brownell, about whom Edward had written to George. Rather than communicate Edward's interest to Sallee, George did all he could to break up any romance. William agreed it was the right thing to do: "Instead of heaping reproaches and execrations on his head, you ought (in

my opinion) render to him the greatest tribute of your gratitude and love." Sallee, it appears, was not a virgin—the letter
is murky at this point, but it is possible that Edward was her
partner. "You say you would not marry for skin now," William
continues. "What else is she good for. I should consider you as
insane indeed if you were to marry a girl that was not virtuous
and had lost her maidenhead."[30]

Double standard for sexual behavior aside, William was
genuinely concerned for his brother and felt the need to repre-
sent his best interests while he was at sea. Edward had "stood
on the verge of an awful precipice and crawled back just in time
to save your neck." Actually, his brothers had done the crawling
back for him. William knows this must hurt: "If I have wrote
anything that will hurt your feelings rest assured it was unin-
tentional. It was to show you your situation which you could
not see (for love has no eyes) rather than hurt your feelings."
When he returned from his second *Cornelia* voyage, Edward
would take an interest in a Miss Brownell, but it would not be
Sallee.

Like all serious whalers, Davoll read the *Whalemen's Shipping
List* whenever it was available. One item in the newspaper while
he was at sea in 1847 might have caught his attention. The article reported that William Brown, second mate of the whaler
Fame of New London, had been arrested for engaging in the
illegal slave trade between Africa and Rio de Janeiro. A young
crewmate, assuming he had shipped on a legitimate whaling
cruise, instead witnessed the *Fame* load more than six hundred
Africans in the hold and transport them to Brazil for sale. His
testimony in federal court led to the arrest of the mate. This
early instance of a slaver disguised as a whaler, from a New
England port, will echo in Edward Davoll's future.[31]

CHAPTER 2

CAPTAIN

When Edward Davoll left his home port of Westport to seek better opportunities in New Bedford, he had set himself on a course to be a career whaleman and, as quickly as possible, to assume command as a master mariner. The late 1840s was a good time to rise in the ranks—there were so many whaling vessels operating out of New Bedford each year that owners and agents were having difficulty finding reliable captains. Edward fit the mold: captains and mates were typically chosen from among "local, native-born white men who went to sea in their mid-teens and quickly worked their way up."[1] Davoll had never been master of a vessel, but he had shown great promise. And, it appeared, he didn't mind being away from home. Since 1840, he had spent a total of seventy months at sea—nearly six of the eight years from age seventeen. He knew whaling, and he knew the *Cornelia,* and he was familiar with the standard routes: the Azores, Cape Verde, the coast of Africa, the Cape of Good Hope, and the Madagascar area of the Indian Ocean. He was just the kind of young man the owners and agents were looking for.

And what was this young man looking for? Having completed two voyages as a foremast hand, one as a boatsteerer, and one as a mate, Davoll would now have the opportunity to be in complete control. After being bossed around for four voyages (progressively less so as he gained rank), he would be the man in charge. And it was nearly total control, with few constraints on his power to determine the course of the voyage, the rules under which the men would live, and the severity of punishment if those rules were transgressed. Certainly, there were limitations: guidelines from the agent and owners; the need to treat men fairly enough to avoid desertions and mutiny; laws regarding punishment, especially flogging; and moral pressure from family and friends at home. No captain wanted to be seen as a tyrant when he was back ashore.

This new position had privileges. Aboard ship he would have a comfortable private cabin, with a steward and cabin boy to wait on him. Beyond the deference afforded to him by the crew—a very small world—he would have status in the wider world. Whaling captains were held in high esteem by the folks back home. And even though he would spend most of his time away, and it was general knowledge that whaling marriages endured severe emotional strains, being a captain enhanced his social standing. He was now a more appealing marriage prospect.

His job alternatives were still the same as when he first went whaling—farming in Westport or factory work in Fall River. Now, with a bit of maritime experience, he might have considered a career as a merchant captain, but by 1850 a whaling captain averaged about $90 per month, three times the average wage of a merchant captain. And whalers always hoped to hit the jackpot with an enormously successful cruise. Perhaps Edward had heard of Nantucket's Obed Starbuck, who in 1830 brought in $50,000 worth of oil on his final voyage and retired at thirty-three.[2]

It was this prospect of early retirement that was most appealing—not a complete withdrawal from work but an end to sea duty and a continuation in the whaling industry as an agent or investor. Captains were often offered part-ownership of the vessel they commanded as a further incentive to fill the hold. This is a key point: a captain did not want to spend the rest of his days at sea. Once he had gained knowledge of the industry and made enough money to buy a house, he preferred a shore-based job associated with whaling, and investing in a variety of whaling voyages was the best way to achieve his goal. A good example of the successful whaling agent is George Howland Sr. of New Bedford. When he died in 1852, his estate was worth $615,000; he had nine whaling vessels, a counting house, a wharf, and a candle factory. His typical profit for a voyage was 6.5 to 14 percent.[3] Davoll would soon be offered the opportunity to invest.

Despite the prospects of wealth, a whaleman's life was lonely and psychologically taxing. It was difficult to sustain relationships with friends and family. And even though his status and income as a captain made him an attractive partner, it was difficult to find a wife or maintain an engagement when absent for two to three years at a stretch. Whaling was perilous, and captains suffered their share of calamities. Just in the eight years that Davoll had been whaling, nineteen New Bedford whaling captains had died at sea, from a variety of causes ranging from being killed by a whale to scurvy to a vessel wrecked in a gale. One died when a man falling from aloft landed on him. In the forty years from 1820 to 1860, there were eighty-eight deaths of New Bedford captains, and in addition to the causes given above can be added heart attack, smallpox, killed in mutiny, killed by South Sea Islanders, and suicide.[4] As the length of voyages increased and whalers extended their geographical range, the statistics got worse—in the coming decade of the 1850s, forty-five New Bedford captains did not return, double the rate of the 1840s.

As Davoll chose to become a captain, a colossal event was taking place on the other side of the continent that would have profound repercussions for New Bedford and the whaling industry. Early in 1848 gold was discovered at Sutter's Mill in California, and rumors began spreading of the opportunity for enormous wealth. Just before Davoll set sail as captain in September 1848, the news hit the East Coast. While he was at sea, whalemen from New Bedford and other ports began flocking to San Francisco—often abandoning their whaling vessels to try their luck. As one New Bedford company wrote to the captain of the whaler *Virginia* early in 1849:

> Since we last wrote you the gold fever has broken out in California. It will subside in less than a year from the time it broke out. Should any of your crew or officers be taken with it, and wish their discharge, by no means comply with their request, but do everything in your power to prevent any of your ships company leaving and more especially your officers. More than ½ the whaling fleet will be withdrawn from the business in the course of the next ensuing 12 months. Therefore all you who hang onto your business . . . will make more gold than any of the diggers in California.[5]

As this letter predicted, most of the men suffering from gold fever would come back empty-handed, but for the next few years prospecting for gold would tempt many in the industry, and Davoll would have to weigh his whaling prospects against the odds of striking it rich in California.[6]

Gold in California was just a shiny rumor when Captain Davoll took command of the *Cornelia* on September 11, 1848. After the customary stop in the Azores, they proceeded down the coast of Africa and into the Indian Ocean. They would have expected to pick up a few hundred barrels of oil as they cruised through whaling grounds along the way, yet when they reported from Fort Dauphin, on the southeast coast of Madagascar on March 19, the ship was "clean." Over the summer, between Madagascar and Johanna Island, they processed 400 barrels. There were no reports through the fall and winter, but by April 1850 they had made their way back around the Cape of Good Hope and were in the Carroll whaling grounds, off the western coast of South Africa, heading for the familiar island of St. Helena, with 780 barrels of sperm oil in the hold.

The *Cornelia* returned to New Bedford on July 18, 1850, carrying 920 barrels of sperm whale oil. At this time, sperm oil was selling for $1.20 per gallon ("The market continues active, and full prices are obtained," wrote the *Whalemen's Shipping List*). At current prices the value of their oil was nearly $36,000. While we don't know the expenses or profit margins for this voyage, it was a good haul for a cruise of less than two years, and Davoll might have earned as much as $2,000. This was certainly a successful first voyage for the young captain—a very promising start.[7]

No log exists for this voyage, and there is only one surviving letter written by Davoll from this time, so aside from the financial success of the cruise, we don't know much about how he did as captain. But there is one unusual document, written at some point in his years as captain, that provides some insight into how he expected a voyage to be conducted and the kind of master he projected himself to be.

Usually on the first day of a voyage, a whaling master assembled the crew and laid out the rules for the cruise. Rarely were these orders written down, and even more rarely would they have survived and ended up in a whaling museum—but Davoll's did. The orders show the captain to have a keen understanding of every role on the ship, from the officers down to the lowliest greenhand. He attempts to draw everyone in to work for a common goal, making it clear who is in charge. "I—and I believe you—come here for the purpose of getting a cargo of oil. To do this there must be a '*head*' or there will be no '*tail*,' or else '*all tail*.' I am here to head and control and conduct the voyage, and you are my co-partners. When I pull I expect you all pull with me, not against me, and when we all pull together with a hearty good will there is easy times for us all and a bountiful harvest in store for our mingled exertions."

This nearly poetic language and high sentiment are balanced with strict rules of conduct for crew members. Foremast hands must "always give a respective answer to every call and order given, day or night, blow high or low. . . . Answer quick. Come quick. Go quick, and do as you are told and you'll find no trouble." No sleeping on watches, no books on deck, no "scrimpshonting" (scrimshanding, or carving scrimshaw) unless he said so. Even grumbling was forbidden: "Grumblers and growlers won't go unpunished." Officers were not to be on friendly terms with the men under their command, and joking with them was specifically forbidden. "In fact," he told them, "the better plan is to never joke at all when at sea, for it generally ends in a quarrel or something similar."

Punishment was an explicit threat. Davoll tells his officers, "I do not want you should be tyrants and brutally treat men, but I do want you should make them know that what you say you mean, and mean what you say." Later he is more direct: "I do not ask you to strike one of the crew. I rather you would not, if you can avoid it, but in case of too tough a cuss, one can't help it once in a while." Of course, discipline was essential on a vessel; in this respect, it was much like a military unit. Davoll comes across as humorless but was probably no more strict than the average whaling master of the era.

The orders weren't all about discipline and punishment. Sundays would be more relaxed, and the men were allowed to read books on deck. There would be "plenty of good and wholesome food" (he claimed), although if any man wasted food he would be put on restricted rations. And the captain could be inspirational as he urged the men to be diligent in spotting whales. "When you are at the masthead on the lookout for whales, sing out for everything that you see. If white water, sing out 'There She White Waters!'; if a breach sing out 'There She Breaches!'; if a spout, sing out 'There She Blows!'; if blackskin, sing out 'There She Blackskins!'; if flukes sing out 'There goes Flukes!'; if a sail sing out 'Sail ho!!' Always sing out at the top of your voices. There is music in it."[8]

Edward Davoll had achieved his goal of master mariner at the age of twenty-five. This was not unheard of (another Westport native, Charles Ball, made captain at twenty-six just a few years earlier), but it was uncommon. This rapid rise through the ranks can be attributed to Davoll's eagerness to learn, willingness to be away at sea for long stretches of time, his well-timed move to New Bedford to take advantage of opportunities that were not available in Westport, and the growth of the whaling industry in general in the 1840s. He had obviously impressed Lemuel Kollock, the New Bedford agent and principal owner of the *Cornelia*. Kollock had first hired him as boatsteerer, then mate on a second voyage, and captain on a third. Davoll had risen on his own merits, a point he would write defensively about later: "I had no better opportunity to get into [whaling] than any other poor fellow. I had no rich parents or influential friends to start me in business. My two hands have been my only helpers."[9]

Certainly, he was proud of his accomplishment. The success of his first cruise as captain proved the rightness of his ambition and the faith that his agent had placed in him. His orders to the crew show that he did indeed have a deep knowledge of every aspect of the operation of a whaling vessel. Yet as the letter quoted above and later letters reveal, he was not entirely comfortable with his position. Making captain at a tender age was laudable, but too fast a rise could also bring jealousy, contempt from more experienced sailors, and self-doubt, however a proud man like Davoll might hide his fears.

It was a difficult role to fill, at any age—daunting, really, as described by the great nineteenth-century chronicler of the whaling industry Alexander Starbuck: "No nobler class of men, no more skillful navigators, ever trod any deck than those who have shipped upon our whalemen. Those in command are brave and daring without recklessness, quick to act in an emergency, but prudently guarding the lives of their men and the safety of their ship; self-reliant but self-possessed."[10]

FIGURE 2. This daguerreotype was probably taken when Edward Davoll first took command of the brig *Cornelia* in 1848. Courtesy of the New Bedford Whaling Museum.

A daguerreotype of Captain Davoll, in formal dress and top hat, with a studio image of a ship in the background, projects a confident man ready to command at sea and to take his place of prominence at home.

We have no firsthand accounts of his initial command, so we can judge Davoll's performance only by results. It was a financially successful voyage with no apparent mishaps, and the owners wanted him back for another. Despite his youth, he now had a confidence-boosting cruise to his credit and would sign on for another command with agent Kollock on the *Cornelia* for a voyage in November. And furthering his long-term goal, he would become part-owner of the *Cornelia,* which means that in addition to his captain's lay, he would take an additional portion of the profits.[11] But as he returned to Westport in July 1850, he had other things on his mind. He was twenty-seven years old, with status and, if not wealth, at least the promise of a healthy income. It was time to get married.

CHAPTER 3

THE PARTING

THE PARTING

We part now, the tenderest friends,
Thou for the ocean main
I in loneliness to stay,
Oh when to meet again.

My heart is sad for thee,
For lone thy way will be, dear,
And oft they tears shall fall,
For thyself and me.

The music of thy gentle voice,
I'l loose for many a year,
And the merry shout of thy approach,
I'l list in vain to hear.

Yet my spirit clings to thee,
Thy soul remains with me,
And oft we'l hold communion sweet,
O'er the dark and distant sea.

And who can paint our mutual joy,
When all thy wanderings o'er,
We both will join in pleasures name,
At home to part no more.

Then gird thine armour on,
Nor faint thou by the way,

Til God shall roll the day around,
When thou shall with me stay.

This poem is in the Davoll Family Papers at the New Bedford Whaling Museum. It is undated, in an envelope addressed in Edward's handwriting to Elizabeth Brownell in Westport. It would have been written in the late 1840s or 1850, before they were married. Because it was sent by Edward, it has been attributed to him. But the point of view of the speaker is that of the person left at home ("I in loneliness to stay"), writing to an absent lover (on "the ocean main").

The professional-quality handwriting matches neither Elizabeth's nor Edward's, suggesting that it was copied in a good hand or that it was written by neither one—an existing poem that matched their sentiments and situation. Various searches have not revealed a poem that exactly matches it, but there are many like it, such as this one printed in *Sailor's Magazine* in 1861:

Thou o'er the world, and I at home—
But one may linger, the other may roam.
Yet our hearts may flee o'er the bounding sea
Mine to thy bosom, and thine to me.[1]

Whether written by Edward or Elizabeth, or copied, "The Parting" does express the situation of a whaling couple who know they are in for a rough time and look forward to the day when they will no longer be apart.

It was obvious to any whaling couple that they would be separated most of the time. For the eighty-two whaling vessels that left New Bedford for the Atlantic, Pacific, and Indian Oceans in 1850, the average duration was three years. One of those voyages lasted more than five years; worse, ten of the ships never returned.[2] Some wives chose to accompany their husbands at sea rather than endure the long separation, but that was relatively uncommon. While Elizabeth Davoll occasionally expressed a wish to join her husband at sea, she remained on land, waiting and hoping. Her marriage would prove challenging.

CHAPTER 4

"KEEP A HIGH TOE NAIL
& A STIFF UPPER LIP"

It was a challenge for a whaling man to find a sweetheart and, if one could be found, to keep her. Long absences made a lonely fiancée consider more accessible options, or at least question the prospect of marriage to a man who would be an absent husband and an unfamiliar father to her children. The girls and women of Westport knew how this worked.

This is not to say that women were averse to marrying a man who had a future in whaling. It was considered an honorable profession, and a captain had status and a good income. Certainly, some women believed that *their* marriage would not follow the old patterns of loneliness, frustration, and disappointment. But even the more realistic ones could look at the absences as temporary: their man would make enough money as captain to retire from the sea and continue working in the industry from the safety and comfort of home. There were sufficient models for this right in Westport, with many fine homes owned by whaling captains, agents, and investors.

As his brother William's letter attests, Edward had chased after women in the brief times between voyages. None had worked out, either of his own choosing or through the interference of his brothers. One young Westport woman, Elizabeth Brownell, had caught his interest sometime before his 1846–48 cruise as an officer aboard the *Cornelia*. Two weeks after returning from that voyage, he had sent her a letter, explaining that he had written so often while at sea "to acquaint you with the regard and esteem I so long had cherished for you . . . and to encourage you to believe what I had written was in sincerity and from pure motives." He writes that the reason he had called on her that evening was "to satisfy myself that you had received my letters written at sea"—an indication that Elizabeth had never answered. Now assured that she was sufficiently interested, he wanted to meet again: "My intentions in regard to the future tense etc., I will explain when more convenient."

Edward suggested they meet the next evening, but added, "If it is not convenient for you to be at home please manifest it by hanging a white handkerchief out of one of the front windows in the west end of the house, to prevent my making inquiry for you. This sight will indicate your absence from home, etc., and I'll pass as if on other business." This letter has many of the markings of stilted nineteenth-century letter writing, but the way he tries to marshal his thoughts ("In the first place . . . Secondly . . . Sixthly") is both comical and endearing. The gist of the letter is: Did you get my letters? I meant what I said; my motives are pure; I still feel the same; let's meet to talk about the future. It takes him four hundred words to get that out. The indirection and awkward phrasing indicate how difficult it must have been for him, a veteran sailor who had encountered enraged fifty-ton whales at close range, to court this young woman seven years his junior. We have no idea how the courtship progressed. Three weeks later he was off to sea again, as captain of the *Cornelia*.[1]

He was away for almost two years. When he returned, in July 1850, he was twenty-seven, an experienced whaling master, and a man of some substance—or at least potential. He was already committed to take the *Cornelia* to the Indian Ocean again in November. During the intervening four months Edward and Elizabeth were married.

Elizabeth Brownell (also known as Libby or Lizzy) was the youngest of four daughters of George C. and Constant Brownell. George was a prosperous farmer, with thirty acres of land under cultivation and seventy more unimproved acres. He raised rye, Indian corn, and oats and kept four milk cows. The total value of his land and livestock was $3,225, making him moderately prosperous by Westport standards. The Brownells lived on the main road connecting the Head of Westport with Howland's Ferry in Tiverton, Rhode Island, and from there to Newport. There were so many Brownell family members in the immediate area that it was called Brownell's Corner. There were a church and a school nearby, but the closest village for shopping and social events was at the Head, two miles distant.

The wedding took place at the Brownell home on September 24, 1850, officiated by Reverend J. B. Parris of the First Christian Church of Westport. Edward had just turned twenty-eight; Elizabeth was twenty-one. Their marriage portraits—miniature photographs in a gold locket—show a pretty woman with dark hair pulled back and fashioned over her ears, looking much younger than her years, and a not-quite-handsome man with dark hair just over his ears and a neatly trimmed "chinstrap" beard (no mustache). Their time together would be short: in two months Edward left to take the *Cornelia* to the Indian Ocean.

An Indian Ocean cruise usually lasted two to three years. Needless to say, this long separation was not the optimal way to start a marriage. Davoll tended to be optimistic about his voyages—his last one had come in under two years, and perhaps he thought this one, with his heightened incentive to return quickly, would be relatively short. An Atlantic cruise would have been shorter but with less potential for a great haul. Davoll could have had a worse assignment: his *Cornelia* agent, Lemuel Kollock, managed four voyages during this time, and they all were distant and potentially very long. One of Kollock's ships, the *Alice Frazier*, was out at the same time in the North Pacific and didn't return for four years.[2] Edward and Elizabeth knew what they were in for, hoped for a very successful short voyage, and, if they were at all realistic, steeled themselves for the worst.

FIGURE 3. Edward Davoll and Elizabeth Brownell were married in their hometown of Westport on September 24, 1850. Photograph courtesy of the locket's owner, Richard Donnelly.

It would be particularly difficult for Elizabeth. The marriage would not live up to the "scripted romantic ideals" of the era, which would cause whaling wives "to experience more deeply an unhappiness with the terms of their own lives."[3] For Edward, the marriage would play a vital role in his decisions about a whaling career. Yet because they were so rarely together, the marriage can be described only obliquely. In some ways, Edward and Elizabeth were more like pen pals corresponding over enormous distances via a highly unreliable postal system of whaling vessels scattered across the world's oceans.

The *Cornelia* set out on November 20, 1850, in its usual route across the Atlantic. There were passengers on board, apparently going to the Azores. Davoll was happy with the ship: "The bark is the best vessel I have ever sailed in. She has the name of a Lady, and she is a Lady like vessel." But ten days out of New Bedford he discovered that one of the passengers had smallpox, and it spread to two crew members. Davoll himself was taken ill, although it is not clear whether he had a mild case of smallpox or some other sickness. Everyone survived, but it could easily have been a disaster. He had not mentioned the "plague" in his earlier letters; only six weeks into the voyage and out of danger did he reveal it to Elizabeth.[4]

And only then could the crew begin whaling. In addition to the smallpox outbreak, gales had been so frequent that they were seldom able to lower boats for whales, and one of their whaleboats had been lost. When they reached the Azorean island of Fayal, they had no oil to show for their Atlantic crossing. Then, instead of proceeding south along the coast of Africa—in the direction of the Indian Ocean—Davoll headed back across the Atlantic to the Caribbean island of St. Vincent. He had received a letter from his agent, Lemuel Kollock, who, after expressing his relief that the captain and crew had survived the smallpox outbreak, recommended that he stay in the Atlantic for eight to ten months before going to the Indian Ocean. Davoll was only too happy to oblige; with luck, he would gather enough oil to make a long Indian Ocean cruise unnecessary. Losing one of his three whaleboats limited the crew's ability to pursue multiple whales at the same time or to converge on a single whale. Kollock said he could send a boat by way of an outbound vessel but thought Davoll would have a better chance of acquiring one from a homebound ship. The agent also advised that if sperm whales were scarce, "try a little whale oil to keep your casks from rotting." But "sperm oil is the stuff [that] makes the money."

Ending on a personal note, Kollock wrote that he had seen Edward's wife and family, and all were well. "No doubt," he wrote, "you will get abundance of letters from them giving all the News about family matters better than I can." But at this point Edward had received no letters from his wife or his family, nor would he for some time. This became a point of frustration and anger as the voyage wore on.[5]

Edward Davoll's career had been on a clear trajectory since he began whaling at seventeen: every voyage had brought him a step closer to his objective, and he reached his goal of master mariner at twenty-five. Now in his second voyage as captain, there was an abrupt change: he no longer wanted to be a whale-man. There were many reasons his change of heart occurred at this particular point. The voyage had started with violent storms and an outbreak of smallpox. The whales he needed for a successful voyage were scarce. But storms, sickness, and scarcity of whales were challenges that captains faced on every voyage. The difference now was that he missed his wife terribly.

"I have resolved within myself to never again separate myself from you and go to sea," he wrote to Elizabeth a few weeks into the cruise.[6] He suggests that next time, she might come with him. Wives did occasionally accompany their captain-husbands, but it was dangerous, lonely with no other female companionship, and often led to pregnancy, which seasickness made harder to endure. Childbirth could be problematic at home, much more dangerous at sea, with the captain as the only "doctor" on board. Expectant mothers were often left on some foreign shore, preferably with women who could assist the childbirth. One Westport woman, Abbie Dexter Hicks, who kept a diary of her time at sea with her husband, had this to say on the day she delivered a baby in a rented house in the Seychelles Islands, while her husband was out to sea: "Baby born about 12—caught two rats."[7] While some crew members appreciated that a captain's wife might have a calming effect on her husband, making their lives a bit easier, most disliked serving on a "hen frigate" because of detours that took time away from whaling and extended their time at sea. So there were many reasons Elizabeth might not see this as an attractive option, and he offered an alternative: "If you do not feel disposed to do so I shall in future try to live the remainder of my days on the land."[8]

And just what would he do on land? He was a young man, only twenty-eight at this point, and had a long working life ahead of him. His best option would be to stay in the whaling industry in another capacity. Like most whaling captains, it had always been his goal to eventually quit the sea and use his master-mariner experience as an agent or outfitter, as well as to invest in whaling vessels and take his share of the proceeds. But that had always been a long way off, and here he was on his second voyage as captain, ready to call it quits.

His emotional state had much to do with the fact that for the first six months of the voyage, he had received no word from Libby. Then, in May, a letter. "Elizabeth! You know not how I prize it. It is the first letter you ever wrote me & the first I have received from home when at sea during the last five years. I would not part with it for a great deal." This of course raises questions: Why had she waited so long to write to her new husband, and why had he not received letters from his family (presumably his parents) in five years? Certainly, mail delivery was unreliable by way of whaling ships, and letters did get lost or long delayed. But that does not entirely account for the fact of his sending so many letters and receiving so few. Libby's unhappiness may have had something to do with it.

Libby's letter was, in fact, not a happy one, as she was having difficulty adjusting to the life of a whaleman's wife. He acknowledged that she was "finding it difficult to bring your mind to your situation." His advice: she must "do as I have done, that is to bring your mind at once to think it is for the best that you & I should be for a season separated. God has seen fit to join us together in Marriage & also to separate us again from each others presence, and if it be his will, we shall meet again in this world, if otherwise I hope it may be in a better world above." There are two important themes expressed here. One is that God is responsible for keeping him away (a refrain he will resort to often, as in "I am resigned to the will of him who has seen fit to afflict me"). The other is that he might not make it back and will be reunited with her only after death. Occasionally, these two refrains are in the same sentence, as when he tells her that the only thing that keeps him going is knowing that "if it is the Will of God for me ever to get home again [she] will receive me with open arms (if living)." These bleak words could not have been comforting to her, but this is how he expressed his growing fatalism about whaling.

We do not have Elizabeth's letter expressing her unhappiness, but from Edward's response it is clear that people back home are talking about him. "Believe not what everybody tells you," he advises.

> Listen not to tales of Gossipers. Heed not what may be said or done to injure your feelings or destroy your happiness. Turn a deaf ear to the babbling of the envious & vicious, whether it concerns you or others, as there are a certain class of people in this world created it seems on purpose, to destroy the happiness of all around them. They are what I call a parcel of busy bodies, who take more interest in others affairs than they do in their own. They go here and there with a pack of Devilish lies on their tongue to create hard feelings one towards another. . . . If everyone would make Mind My Own Business their Motto we would see peace & harmony both at home and abroad.

This will also become a theme, that others are jealous of his rapid rise to captain and are poisoning his wife's mind. Right now, with distance and time working against him, all he can do is tell her to toughen up: "You must do as I do, that is carry a high toe nail & a stiff upper lip."[9] And to some degree it appears that she was doing something about her situation: learning to play the piano. "Libby has got to playing Old Dan Tucker," Davoll's brother-in-law reported, "and will be able to play all the most popular tunes of the day soon."[10]

The gossip from home apparently bothered Edward as much as it did Libby, and he defensively returned to the subject two weeks later. His letter begins with his characteristic self-pity, longing for the day when "I shall once more rid my-self of the cares which beset those in my present situation, and once more join with you in the many privileges enjoyed on the land, which for the chief of the last twelve years I have scarcely had a claim." But then he attacks the "Land Lubbers" who (he believes) consider whalemen to have an easy life. "They will say he has nothing to do but lounge about the decks, Eat, Sleep, Smoke his Pipe & tell Stories. Just let them try it once, and then if they do not sing a different tune I am sadly mistaken." The fact that these "confounded lies" got under his skin suggests that he was still insecure in his role as captain.[11]

Even though whales were more plentiful in July as the *Cornelia* sailed through the Caribbean to the Bahama Banks, the captain was upset that he had received no more than that single letter from Libby. Crew members had received mail by way of a ship that had recently left Westport; how could she have failed to send a letter that was sure to get to him? He reprimands her, then apologizes. A few days later when another ship brings mail, he boils over: "I would give $20 to have a good letter from you and $10 to have a good one from almost anyone else."[12] The distress of not getting mail at sea is real, but we can only guess at the reasons. Was his wife too depressed to write? Was he estranged from his parents? Had he alienated his friends? In his despondent mood he reconsiders one of his moneymak-ing options: "I as much thought of being in California Gold Digging as I did of being where I am."[13]

He found another reason to be angry. He was convinced that his third mate, Walton Delano, was the reason for the poor whaling so far. As he explains to Libby, "This worthy Gentleman in the first place is a notorious Drunkard, in the 2nd an infernal Villain, 3dly is guilty of thieving, lying, and is the whole cause of my not having 300 bbls sperm oil to send home instead of what I do [120 barrels]." Davoll doesn't explain just how Delano was responsible for this, but since each mate usually led one of the whaleboat crews, he may have botched the capture of several whales. The captain spends more time explaining how Delano had led the steward, George Russell, to drink. This was family news, as George was the brother of Holder Russell, the husband of Libby's sister Clarissa. "George is a good boy," he assures his wife, and after a good talking-to by the captain had promised not to be led astray again. After passing on this family gossip, Edward asks Libby not to tell George's parents, although it seems unlikely that any news in a whaleman's infrequent correspondence remained a secret.[14]

By the late summer of 1851, the *Cornelia* was heading back to the Azores. Davoll now had to admit that whaling in the Atlantic would not produce the results he needed, and he would have to resort to the original plan of cruising in the Indian Ocean. After expressing his delight in receiving three letters from Libby, he tells her he will be away much longer. "I do not want to cause you any unpleasant feelings & I hope you will not be simple enough to let it trouble you when I tell you that I cannot think of coming home anything short of a good voyage." His desire to be with her was overmatched by his sense of responsibility to the owners, but also his own pride: "Remember that I do not want people to say that Ned Davoll has come home again & made a poor voyage." He softens the message to Libby by adding that this voyage will be "my last one in the Whaling business." He will fill the *Cornelia's* hold "so as to bid adieu to Whaling ever more." He might stay in the maritime business but in shorter trading voyages rather than whaling and would take Elizabeth with him. It seems that this plan has eased his mind; he reports he is blessed with "good health, a fair appetite for eating & sleeping, smoking & chewing tobacco, telling stories with the mates and Boatsteerers. And to crown all to read over the letters I have received from you." He sounds a bit more at peace here, not the friendless and disappointed man he so often projects in his letters.[15]

In September 1851 the *Cornelia* pulled into Horta, on the Azorean island of Fayal, to repair a broken windlass (a winch for pulling up the anchor). The captain sent the ship out whaling under the command of Mr. Crapo, the first mate, while he stayed on shore to monitor the repair. "The Portuguese are so thick headed that I have been obliged to stay here and watch them that they might perform the work well." While there, he heard that the mate had taken a whale, "but I cannot put confidence in the report because it was made by a Portuguese." This casual prejudice is perhaps only too common to the age and at this point not enough to brand Davoll as particularly bigoted.

On shore at Fayal he got to socialize with several other whaling captains, an opportunity to relax from the responsibilities of shipboard command and to catch up on industry news and gossip from home. Unfortunately, some of the captains were accompanied by their wives, making Davoll feel, as he reported to Libby, "lonesome as death."[16] The prospect of his wife joining him would come up again a few months later when Edward crossed paths with Captain Frederick Crossman of the Westport brig *Leonidas,* who had spoken with Libby and reported that she wanted to get on the next ship to be with her husband. Oddly, after expressing that very desire so many times, Davoll demurred. "I am of the opinion that your heart would fail you in making such an attempt," he wrote. Whether she was in poor health or, in his opinion, couldn't stand the rigors of the voyage, we don't know. Why, if he was so lonely, wouldn't he want her to join him? "I should advise you to remain where you are, for the *Cornelia,* about now, is rather greasy," meaning they were processing whale blubber. It appears that, despite his acute loneliness, he was ambivalent about having his wife on board. All he wanted Libby to do was to "fervently pray for my success" so that he would "have something to jingle [that is, money in his pocket] after I get Home."[17]

~~~~~~~

Having made the decision to continue the voyage to the Indian Ocean, Davoll steered south toward Cape Verde and St. Helena and by January 1, 1852, reached Tristan da Cunha, deep in the South Atlantic and a regular resupply stop before attempting the treacherous passage around the Cape of Good Hope. He wrote to Libby as he was leaving Tristan. Now over a year into the cruise, the whaling had improved somewhat, with 120 barrels of sperm oil and 65 of "black oil" (from right whales) in addition to what he had already off-loaded in the Azores. (Masters often unloaded oil when there was access to a market or shipping facility in order to make room in the hold for more oil as the voyage continued.) He had seen only two sperm whales since last July but captured both, "which shows that we can get the Buggers if we can see them." He had heard that Elizabeth's father was near death and her mother not doing well either and could only resort to a religious bromide: "God giveth and God taketh away blessed be the name of the Lord." By this time her father, George Brownell, had already died, on September 22, 1851, at age sixty-seven. In his will he left his wife all their household furniture and $3,000—an indication of their moderate wealth. Elizabeth and her sisters would equally share "all the rest, residue, and remainder of [his] estate."[18]

The captain now predicted that the voyage would be two and a half, possibly three, years in duration. This was not good news for Elizabeth, nor was his remark that he will see her again only "if life be spared," another instance of the fatalism that increasingly crept into his letters. Money, of course, was the goal of any whaling voyage, but now he begins to calculate his captain's portion and owner's share not with living expenses in mind but retirement. "I have made or have taken oil enough so that my lay & vessel's share brings me at the rate oil is selling for now rising $100.00 per month, which is better than nothing." It was, in fact, just about average.[19] "I cannot think of coming home with anything less than 1000 bbls Sp[erm] oil," he writes, "& I am in hopes of getting 1200 so as to bid adieu to

Whale fishing after this voyage."[20] This is far more than the 500 barrels he had originally projected. He was now pressing on for an extraordinarily successful voyage that would allow him to retire from a life at sea.

By March 1852 he had rounded the Cape of Good Hope and entered familiar territory, cruising around Madagascar and in the Mozambique Channel up to Johanna Island. Although well known to Davoll from previous voyages, the area could not have been entirely comfortable. The previous year the *Queen of the West,* a schooner from his neighboring town of Dartmouth, Massachusetts, had been collecting tortoise shells at Madagascar when the crew was killed and the vessel burned by natives of the island.[21] When whaling in the area, it was occasionally necessary to go ashore for fresh water and vegetables, and the men often demanded shore leave after months at sea. Whether Captain Davoll allowed the men liberty on Madagascar, as the crew of the New Bedford whaler *Wave* did that year, to enjoy "the ladies of pleasure [who are] dark as mid night and for 2 yards of 5 cent cotton they afford all their charms which are verry few," is unknown.[22] On later voyages Davoll would have to deal with crew members who contracted venereal disease.

In a letter to the *Whalemen's Shipping List* newspaper in March 1852, the captain relayed discouraging news from two other New Bedford whalers that he had encountered at Madagascar. The *Milwood* had seen eleven whales in the past month but caught none. And the *Messenger* "had lost her cooper, who jumped overboard in a fit of insanity and was drowned."[23] He had now been out for more than two years but felt obligated to remain in the Indian Ocean until he had met the quota on which he and the agent had agreed. "I put her [*Cornelia*] in for 1000 bbls on board before I start for home," he explained to Elizabeth in March. If he did not return with a full load, it would show "a timid spirit with a fickle mind and doubting heart." He wants to make it clear that this is not him: "I despise a coward, scorn a fickle mind, deride a doubting heart."[24] This is how he justifies to his wife why he will be away longer than either of them wants, but it is also a classic example of his proud and defensive side. Other captains might shrink from their duty to stay out until the hold is filled, but not Captain Davoll!

In this same letter of March 26, 1852, he vents to his wife about a family matter that upset him. He received news of various babies being born to family members, including his younger brother George. His reaction: "I say that all who are so fond of having a large brood of snotty nosed urchins to Support & Educate them in a proper manner." This suggests some bitterness that he and Libby as yet had no children. They had spent only two months together during nearly three years of marriage—just one more thing to feel inadequate or frustrated about while far from home.

Despite the brave front—no fickle mind or doubting heart—he was having trouble facing up to his duties. In June he admits, "I cannot get my mind steady for I have been in a perfect confusion for the past week by the natives. They are enough to make a man seem mad." An American trading crew had recently been massacred by natives on Minow Island on the southwest coast of Madagascar. The natives had been trading on board, saw some valuables, and then killed the crew and plundered the ship. Sharing this danger with Libby might have provided some relief to him, but it could not have eased her mind, particularly as she had been ill. Health is everything, he tells her. "Rob me of everything else but my wife & my health & I can get along, but if either of them are lost I am undone. Particularly the former."[25]

Whales remained scarce. In June 1852 he reported only 25 barrels (probably one small whale) since February. "I am almost ready to believe there is no whales alive. Sill there must be some, somewhere." As he often did when disheartened, he places the onus for his situation on the Almighty: "I would to God I was there [with Libby] tonight, but he has decreed it otherwise and I must be content with my lot." Characteristically, he adds that he would never leave her, "if I am fortunate enough to get home to you again." He says this often enough to suggest that he feared he would not survive the voyage.

The captain ended this June 7 letter by advising his wife about her living situation, which was with her sister Hannah and brother-in-law Perry G. Lawton. Apparently, Libby had suggested living elsewhere, perhaps in a rented space of her own. Edward recommended she stay put, because Perry was able to take care of her. In the whaling mythology of the era, captains owned their own homes and provided a stable living situation for their families. True, Davoll was on only his second voyage as master, and they had been married only two years, but she was living with her sister and had no prospects of doing otherwise.[26]

For the remainder of 1852 and into the following year, the *Cornelia* cruised in a constrained area between Madagascar and the Comoro archipelago to the north. From Johanna Island (present-day Anjouan) he reported 250 barrels of sperm oil in May, from Comoro Island 300 barrels in August, and from the Mozambique Channel 400 barrels in October. There were no reports of further catches through the winter months.

In early April 1853, with only 400 of the 1,000 barrels of sperm whale oil he had vowed to return with, the captain left the Indian Ocean and headed for home. He would pass through several Atlantic whaling grounds, so there could be more, but it was clear that this would not be the voyage to end all (his) voyages. They had some luck as they proceeded to St. Helena and on to the Azores. Davoll's estimate of thirty to thirty-six months was accurate. When the pilot guided the *Cornelia* into New Bedford harbor on August 26, 1853, they had been out for thirty-three months.

What they had to show for it was 547 barrels of sperm oil and

270 of whale oil. They also brought in 2,200 pounds of whale-bone. Normally, sperm whalers did not bother with whale-bone because sperm whales have teeth rather than baleen, but since the *Cornelia* crew had taken quite a few right whales, they would also harvest the baleen while they were at it. At about 34 cents per pound in 1853, this would have amounted to only $750, a small percentage of their total catch. At then current prices, the gross income for the cruise totaled about $27,000.[27]

Aside from the total income, there are no specific figures for this voyage, so we can only approximate Captain Davoll's earnings based on averages that have been calculated for the period.[28] His captain's lay would have amounted to about $1,800. Partial ownership sometimes brought in as much as a captain's lay, so Davoll's two-sixteenths share was likely worth $1,000 or more. A rough estimate, then, would bring his earnings to $3,000.[29] This would have been considered a good haul, except for the fact that the captain had wanted this to be his last whaling voyage and it had come in at about half his goal. But it did allow him to stay at home for a year. The absence of letters from this period makes it impossible to know what he was thinking, but we can assume that, in addition to simply enjoying the company of his wife whom he had seen for only two months in the past three years, he gave serious thought to other kinds of work within the whaling industry or "almost any kind of business on the land."[30]

Being home for a full year was unusual for a man who rarely spent more than a couple of months between voyages. It is not surprising that his wife soon became pregnant, but veteran mariners were rarely home for both conception and childbirth. Edward was one of the lucky ones and was there for the birth of their daughter, Carrie Clinton Davoll, on August 10, 1854. His money problems were not resolved, however, and despite his grand plans to quit whaling, he would be with his new child for only twelve days before it was time to leave for his next long voyage to the Indian Ocean.

CHAPTER 5

THE WRECK OF THE *IRIS*

It is about ten miles from the center of Westport to the wharves of New Bedford, two hours or so by horse. On August 22, 1854, Edward Davoll left his wife and newborn daughter, who were staying with Libby's mother, and rode to New Bedford to take command of the whaling bark *Iris*. Captains did not sail their large vessels out from the harbor; that was the job for a pilot, who guided the *Iris* out and anchored off Clark's Point. Davoll then took over and sailed only four miles "when the wind all died away to a calm." The tide was against them, and rather than drift back toward shore they anchored again. When the breeze came up it was very strong, and the captain was "verry glad that we came to an anchor." Later in the day his brother-in-law Holder Russell, a temporary visitor on the ship, took a boat to shore, which was an opportunity for the captain to return to Westport for the night. Instead, he wrote to Libby, explaining that "I chose to remain on board for if I went on Shore all the Officers & Boatsteerers and probably most of the Crew would have wanted to. I would like to be with you to night but as I am on board the ship Comfortably Situated with a good Steward to provide Good Meals I choose remaining on board, that is for to night. Tomorrow if the weather is not suitable for us to go to sea I may go on Shore."[1]

"I do dread coming out to Westport because it is so verry hard to part," he went on, defensively, sure that Libby would blame him for preferring to stay aboard rather than travel that ten miles to be with her and their daughter. "Don't say I am hard hearted," he pleaded. He felt it was his duty to be with his ship, and maybe that's all there was to it. Davoll certainly exhibited a devotion to duty throughout his career. But it could have been that this man, used to command, needed to remove himself from his in-law's home and a fussy newborn baby—a situation that he could not control.

The following day he wrote again: "Wednesday Morn has dawned and the weather is fine." He was waiting for the pilot to take the *Iris* out again. "I hope he will come soon for I want to be moving." Then the letter turns to money matters. Davoll worried that he had not adequately covered the cost of the hired horse that carried him from Westport to New Bedford. He was touchy on the subject of money: "God forbid my owing a cent and not pay." Continuing with finance, he tells Libby, "Don't be to[o] much for keeping money, use it, for it is made for that purpose. Supply all your wants if Money will pay for them." He advises her to keep Mrs. Luce (probably the woman who helped with the baby) for as long as needed. "Don't Exert yourself too much, remember the condition of Mrs. King," apparently someone who did not take care of herself after giving birth. "Keep up good Spirits and bear in mind that there is one who lives for you & you only."

Given his growing disillusionment with whaling and the further strain on his marriage with a new child to provide for, going back out to sea for two years was difficult. Failing in his goal of having a place of their own, he reiterates a promise he had begun making on the *Cornelia*: "My mind now is to live in a different manner from what we have since we was married when I return. I want a home of my own and if I can come to you again you may rest assured that I will be the owner of a residing place. I don't like this hanging out."

But then it is back to business. "I feel first rate this morning. I can go to sea with a willing heart for I feel it my duty to do so. I have great confidence of making a good voyage." He

FIGURE 4. The whaling bark *Iris* was built in Westport in 1818. Under Captain Davoll's command in 1855, the *Iris* was wrecked in a storm on the west coast of Australia. This painting was made by Richard E. Norton, first mate on an earlier voyage of the *Iris*. From the Collections of the Martha's Vineyard Museum.

then adds, "I think I have a nice Sett of Officers & a smart set of Men for a crew." Later events will force him to reconsider those observations.[2]

The *Iris* was a 311-ton three-masted bark, almost one hundred feet along the deck. In tonnage and length, it was the largest vessel that Davoll had commanded up to this point. By coincidence, it had been built in Davoll's hometown of Westport in 1818, four years before he was born. The *Iris* was a veteran of thirteen whaling voyages, all in the Pacific and Indian Oceans. Now, under its thirty-two-year-old master, it would once again sail for the Indian Ocean, a destination that Davoll had been to three times before, most recently as captain of the *Cornelia*.

The first stop was Fayal, in the Azores, a place familiar to Davoll. He wrote to Libby on September 28 from "his old boarding place" that he had bought her two bonnets, a veil, and a hair tie that he will send to her (he estimates they will arrive by November). He lists how much each item cost and claims he would have bought more "if I had plenty Money . . . but according to present circumstances I do not think it propper."[3] So far he had only 25 barrels of sperm oil to show for his five weeks at sea but decided to unload it at Fayal.

At next report, December 7, the *Iris* was at Tristan da Cunha, a common provisioning stop for whaling vessels fifteen hundred miles west of South Africa. "No oil," Davoll reports. From there it was sixty-five hundred miles of open water, past the Cape of Good Hope (whose original name, Cape of Storms, attests to the severe weather sailors typically encountered there) to Western Australia.[4] Like many mariners, Davoll referred to Australia as "New Holland," even though the name was several decades officially out of date. Whaling improved a bit on this leg of the journey, and by early March, when the *Iris* reached King George's Sound off the southwestern coast of Australia, it had 150 barrels of sperm oil on board.[5] The rest of the voyage would add nothing to that total.

In March 1855 he wrote to Libby, responding to news of the "Cold, Cold Winter" she had experienced back in Massachusetts. He longed to be home to share the "many uncomfortable & dreary hours which if I could have been with you, might in many instances been alleviated. But God has ordered it otherwise." Edward always had a tendency to use ornate or flowery language, but now he waxes poetic as he anticipates Libby's enjoyment of the coming summer: "The intensity of Cold & howling storms will then depart for days when all Nature is gay. The Birds will warble their Sweet Notes to you, the trees put forth and blossom, the Sun shine radiantly on hill & dale, giving life & beauty to all around you. Methinks I can hear you singing sweetly to little Carrie caressing her into slumbers of sweet repose."

There was also more advice on child rearing: "Administer to her all things needful, but not lavish to[o] many Extravagances for fear such indulgences in future may be regretted." He then moves on to Libby's health, admonishing her to "always avoid Exposure" and to "get Some One to do your washing and ironing for it gives me pain to think that you are disposed to do it yourself." She must not, "for a few paltry dollars," disregard her health. Apparently, he considered her immature in this regard: "You are now a 'Woman,' therefore don't act as little Girls."

The rest of this long letter is about finances and provides some insight into his business arrangements. He engaged his wife in these matters for two reasons: one was the role she could play in managing their affairs, and the other was to duplicate instructions that he had sent to a Westport agent, Christopher Church, "in case the letter be miscarried"—a common occurrence given the complications of mail delivery to and from whaling vessels across the globe. Libby's role in her husband's absence, as he clearly laid out, was to receive any payments due him and sign and date all receipts, "so that there will be no trouble (in case of his [Church's] death) in making a settlement." Her role was lessened when it came to getting money from his New Bedford agent, Lemuel Kollock; she was to "have Perry, my Father, or some trusty relatives have the Notes & collect the money." There were limits to Libby's management of the family finances, even during a two-year absence.

She could play a sort of lobbying role, however. Davoll wanted to sell his two shares of the *Cornelia*, which he had owned since 1848, and Libby was to relay this to Mr. Church and "encourage the sale of the vessel if he can get a fair price for her." While she was interacting with Church, however, she was not to let on to him what might be going on with agent Kollock. Church owned a store at the Head of Westport, near the Davoll family home, and had been active in town government—including collector of taxes. Davoll wanted to keep from Church any knowledge of his income from other sources. "I do not want C. A. Church or any one that has anything to do with Town affairs to know anything about the Money that Mr. Kollock owes me, on account of being taxed for it."[6]

As someone whose entire career had been in one industry,

his only hope of a land job was dependent on leveraging his experience as a master whaler to manage and invest in whaling voyages, and that is why his *Cornelia* stake matters. He was trying to decide whether holding on to his shares and receiving a cut of the profit from the *Cornelia*'s next voyage would be a better deal than selling and investing the proceeds elsewhere. In this case, he thought selling would be the better bet but deferred to Church's judgment. His goal was to be in Church's place—dealing with the financial aspects of whaling voyages from the comfort and safety of home or office on dry land.

Wives often played a critical role in managing the family finances while their husbands were away at sea. The Davoll marriage fit another pattern, that of the husband dictating the terms and the wife following that advice and relying on men on shore—father, brothers, agents—to help her. Elizabeth seems to have played a secondary role in the family economy, a weak financial partner to her husband. Since we have no letters from Elizabeth to Edward, we have no way of knowing if that is the role she preferred: whether she had expressed an inability or unwillingness to be more involved in financial matters or if it was a role imposed on her by her husband.[7]

March 1855 marked the six-month point in the voyage, and with 150 barrels of oil (plus 25 barrels he had left at Fayal) the captain knew he was behind expectations. He did not blame this poor showing on the crew, which he continued to praise: "I have, as far as I can see, a first rate sett of Officers, good Boatsteerers & a good quiet peaceable crew." The problem was the dearth of whales sighted. They had "seen Sperm Whales but 3 times since leaving the Western Islands [Azores] & only 4 times since leaving Home." Davoll foresaw "nothing preventing my making a good Voyage," but estimated it would take an additional two years to reach his goal. This cannot have been good news for his wife: their daughter, Carrie, would be two and a half years old before seeing her father again.[8]

In April, as he cruised the southern coast of Australia, Davoll wrote a long character-revealing letter to Elizabeth. With little exchange of personal information, or response to her most recent letter, or asking for family and friends back home—as he typically did—he essentially wrote a review of a book titled *Queechy,* by Elizabeth Wetherell. In mid-nineteenth-century America, Wetherell (the pen name of Susan Warner) was a famous writer of religious fiction and almost as well known as her contemporary Harriet Beecher Stowe.[9] Davoll went on at length about the young heroine of the novel, Elfleda or Fleda, a model of Christian conduct. Like Eva in Stowe's best seller from the same era, *Uncle Tom's Cabin,* Fleda is simply too good to be true. Davoll had borrowed the book from another captain and, without actually reading it ("as far as I have browsed it"), tells Libby, "I can truly call it a very good book & strongly recommend you to come into possession of the same good work as soon as possible."

The moral lessons of the book are intended for their daughter, Carrie. "Why I write you this is because I wish you to instill into our sweet 'Babe' the same character which Elfleda possesses, & that she may be as bright an ornament in the world, God forbid her being otherwise." To Davoll, Fleda is "the model of perfection . . . in Pity, truth & innocence." Libby must "endeavor to make her another 'Fleda' in every respect," to form a character that will go with her "to the Grave, unblemished & unspotted."

Elizabeth had little say in the matter. "You will, of course, avail yourself of the first opportunity to become in possession of the Book called 'Queechy,' & read the same as I am very desirous that our Little 'Carrie' shall be not only to us, but to others also, one of the sweetest of children. . . . Hoping and trusting that you will in no wise do anything short of making her what 'Fleda' in the Book is." He even tells her which New Bedford bookstore to go to or to send to Boston or New York if it is unavailable locally. "I sincerely hope you will lose no time in getting it. I know you will like it & thank me for giving you the information of the treasure."[10]

Most of Davoll's letters are relatively conversational in style, at least by nineteenth-century standards, but this letter is unusually stilted in language, apparently to impress on his wife that he meant business but more that he was in a cultural position as her husband to dictate what she must do. Phrases like "avail yourself of the first opportunity to become in possession of" rather than "get" are indications of pompous language to impress her of his mastery.

His understanding of the proper conduct of women combines with his sense of command in this effort to control his wife's behavior from the distance of twelve thousand miles. He also expresses strong opinions on parenting, even though he has seen his only child for a total of twelve days. By the middle of the nineteenth century, earlier concepts of seafaring men being in command both at sea and at home had given way to the idea that men and women belonged to different spheres—men dominating the world of work and women in control at home. But here Edward Davoll still behaved like an eighteenth-century whaleman, directing the "domestic sphere" from aboard ship. True, these were difficult transitions, as ideas about family and relationships "developed in painful contradiction to the material circumstances of their lives and were stretched beyond plausibility."[11] It was as if Edward believed that nothing had changed from the earlier days of whaling, when shorter voyages meant that men could maintain a dominant role in domestic life, and the 1850s, when the lengthening of voyages to two to four years meant a transformation of roles in which men ceded domestic control to their wives.

His strongly stated religious views are consistent with earlier letters—and fairly typical of the nineteenth century. He was, to all appearances, a devout Christian. But the rigid morality expressed in this letter not only makes him appear insufferable (at least to modern sensibilities) but also creates a stark contrast to some of the moral decisions that he will make in the near future.

While we might find his writing style self-righteous and annoying, we do have to be aware of his circumstances. This pompous man can elicit sympathy, if we understand what the world looks like to him. Whales are scarce. He writes letters that take months (if ever) to reach home and receives very few from his wife and family. In March 1855 he complained that he had not received any news from home since leaving the Azores—a period of five months. Through the pretentious language ("I should be very happy indeed to have the pleasure of perusing a few lines from your hand") comes a forlorn soul in need of someone to care for him. He doesn't even know if Libby received the bonnets he sent her from the Azores so many months ago. He was genuinely lonely without his wife and daughter and had not expected to be still toiling so far from home for so long. But now rather than lash out at all those who don't write, as he often did in the past, he simply bears it as best he can: "I carry a high toe nail & a stiff upper lip."

In a brief respite from the sea, Davoll made a visit to Port Albany, on the southwestern coast of Australia, and described the place to Libby. Settled by the British in 1827, Albany's deep-water port made it a suitable stop for large numbers of whalers in the southern Australian waters. He was impressed with the beautiful "English" settlement of Albany and asks his wife to imagine "a fine Smooth Sheet of water surrounded by High rocky & Mountainous land . . . [and] Ships laying to anchor near the Western Shore which rises by degrees to Mountainous heights. At the foot of the heights bordering on a white sand beach stands a few dwelling Houses and Stores, a Prison, Courthouse, Church, etc." There were about three hundred inhabitants— "English, Irish & Scotch with one or two Americans."

But another sight he found appalling. "In the vicinity of the town there are about 200 or 300 of the most Filthy and

Mizerable Native Blacks I ever beheld. They live in little Huts about 6 feet in diameter which are made in a circular form with an opening large Enough for one to crawl in at a time, from 6 to 8 take lodgings in one of these Huts at a time. Their Dress is made of Kangaroo Skins which they make fast around their Necks Hair Side Next to their Skins, which covers their Bodies only, their legs going entirely bare & their Heads have no covering more than a Matted Mess of Hair which grows in great profusion."

"Their food," he continues, "consists of Worms, Snakes, all Manner of Bugs & fish. They are said to be remarkably fond of Carrion of all Kind." On the positive side, they are expert at throwing a spear and are "inoffensive and stand in great fear of White people." But his overall opinion is unequivocal: "One cannot look at them without being disgusted." After watching them dance, he adds, "I could not bear to look at such horrid dirty objects only for a few moments."[12]

What can we make of these comments? Some of his opinions were preformed ("I had heard of their disgusting appearance before"), so he had a prejudgment to which he could now add his personal observations. We could not expect him to have the objectivity of an anthropologist seeing a foreign culture for the first time. Yet there is something callous about his comments; he essentially apologizes to Libby, "knowing full well that it cannot interest you much but I have nothing else to write about." It must be said that this attitude toward foreign cultures and people of color was commonplace at the time and not surprising for a man who held the Portuguese of the Azores in such low esteem. Yet the phrase "horrid dirty objects" is hard to forget and suggests a deeply felt racial prejudice.

Lingering in Albany was not an option, as the hold of the *Iris* was less than a quarter filled with oil. From April 1 to June 1, Davoll cruised off the southern coast in company with the *Congress*, the *Lapwing*, the *Martha*, the *Draco*, and two dozen other whalers. The captain had "heard of no other ships doing

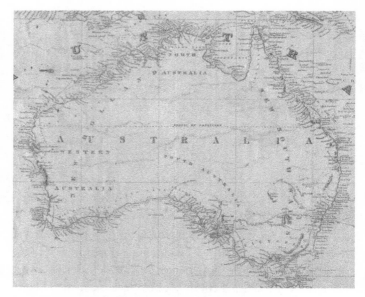

FIGURE 5. Captain Davoll still referred to Western Australia by its former name, New Holland. Along the southwest coast is Albany, where Davoll first encountered Aborigines. Farther up the west coast, the *Iris* was shipwrecked in a storm in 1855. Map courtesy of the New Bedford Whaling Museum.

anything; whales very scarce."[13] He decided to leave this congested area and proceeded northerly along the coast of Western Australia. In a later letter to the *Whalemen's Shipping List,* he explained that his intention was to put in at Port Gregory, about three hundred miles north of Perth, to hunt humpback whales. He made no mention of a problem with his ship, but other sources indicate that the *Iris* had sprung a leak and Port Gregory was the most convenient place to pull in. The plan was to "careen" the ship—run it onto a sandy shore at high tide so that it would lie to one side, exposing the hull on the damaged side for repair.[14]

Aside from the matter of the leak, there is agreement on what happened next. At three o'clock on the morning of July 10, 1855, while the *Iris* was securely anchored, Davoll reported, "a very severe gale from the north west sprung up, and accompanied with a strong current, [the *Iris* was] driven ashore. The ship lies deeply embedded in the sand, and will undoubtedly prove a total loss." The captain and crew pitched tents on the beach and began unloading the ship, both to save the cargo and equipment and to lighten the load in an attempt to refloat the vessel. William Burges, the resident magistrate, placed a constable at the scene "to see that no robbing shall be committed and that no goods liable to duty shall be landed without my knowledge." Despite the crew's efforts, they were unable to free the *Iris,* which was condemned by the Board of Survey, the official government inspectors for the Colony of Western Australia.[15]

Captain Davoll's duty now was to salvage anything of value from the wreck of his ship. There were 150 barrels of sperm whale oil, which he sent to London to be sold. Davoll also reported that he had one humpback whale, apparently not yet rendered into oil, although humpback oil was of much lower quality than sperm oil, and the baleen was not very valuable. The *Iris* also had a great deal of rigging, sails, and equipment that was auctioned off in October. Whaling gear was very much in demand in Australia, so this proved to be a valuable asset, though hardly recompense for what was decidedly a failed voyage.[16]

That failure weighed heavily on a very angry crew. Davoll had commented back in March that he had a "first rate sett of Officers," but now the first mate, Ephraim C. Ellis, was giving him trouble. Crews would be paid only if a voyage was profitable, and this one certainly would not be. Unless they could secure a berth on another whaling vessel, they would have to endure several more months without pay on their return home, their only hope being compensation from the U.S. consul at Fremantle. The crew (including the officers) threw themselves on the mercy of Burges, the local magistrate: "Sir we the undersigned officers and crew of the ship *Iris* wrecked this port on the 10th July 1855 being now left destitute without means of proceeding elsewhere do throw ourselves in your hands as the Representative of the British Government here, praying that you will forward us to our respective consuls."[17]

Burges contacted Thomas Pope, the American consul at Fremantle. Although originally from New Bedford, Pope proved to be of little help. For example, he felt no need to aid any of the Portuguese crew members, despite the fact that he was responsible for American seamen and "regularly hired seamen on board an American vessel." Burges informed the captain that the consul had made no arrangements for the crew and placed the burden back on Davoll. "We now call on you to furnish rations from the stores saved from the ship to the maintenance of 27 men including officers who are now proceeding to Fremantle in schooner *Perseverance* to claim protection of the US Consul. Rations will include 337 lbs salt pork, 236 lbs bread, 60 lbs sugar and 9 lbs tea also sufficient wood for the cooking of these rations."[18]

The intent here seems to be that the food salvaged from the ship should go to the crew rather than be sold for the benefit of the owners and investors. There is no record of who paid for the crew's rations, but in any event twenty-seven of the crew left Port Gregory on the *Perseverance* and made their way to Fremantle, where they would hope for some assistance from the consul.

The captain sums up the crew's resentment in a letter to his wife: "The mate is at the bottom of this affair." The mate may in fact have aggravated the crew's displeasure, but it was natural to blame the man whom they had trusted to bring the ship home safely with a hold full of oil. There had been no apparent ill feeling before the incident: he had recently commented about the quality of his officers and the peaceable nature of the crew, so their anger does not appear to be a holdover from any mistreatment during the voyage.[19]

But was it Davoll's negligence that led to the shipwreck? Before the gale, he had secured the ship "on good holding ground with two anchors ahead, a kedge [light anchor] and moving buoy

astern." The resident magistrate's report suggested unusual circumstances. "It was during a heavy gale from NW and strange
to say the current carried her out against the wind, and the anchors seemed to drift faster than the vessel as if the whole bottom of the anchorage bodily gave way. She had an anchor out
astern and it, all the time she was dragging, kept a strain on the
cable. She went out stern foremost and had three anchors out,
one of which came foul of the mooring chains of the large buoy,
and all went away together." So it is likely that the captain had
done everything a master mariner should have done and that he
wasn't to blame for the accident. It is also possible that the *Iris*
was not as badly damaged as assessed by the Board of Survey,
because after the ship was condemned it was purchased at auction and refloated in January 1855. The renamed *Frances* sailed for
at least another ten years in the merchant trade.

Another possibility is that the Australian authorities might
have intentionally condemned a salvageable vessel, due to resentment of all the American ships and aggressive captains in
their waters. It was a record year for whaling in 1855, with 466
New England vessels cruising the seas, mostly in the Pacific
and Indian Oceans.[20] (The "20 or 30" ships Davoll mentioned
in company with the *Iris* off King George Sound attest to the
overabundance of whalers in Australian waters.) Captain
Davoll was certainly at a disadvantage, far from home and with
the nearest American consul three hundred miles away, and
he was forced to accept the decision of local authorities. But
regardless of the actual condition of the ship, Davoll was the
master, and ultimate blame for the mishap fell on his shoulders.
He had let down the owners, the investors, and the crew, and
this could only be seen and felt as a severe personal and professional embarrassment.

Davoll always expressed a great sense of duty in his letters; here
he adds a tone of self-pity: "I have undergone almost everything a Man can endure in order to save the cargo which I have

accomplished to the best of my abilities but if you only knew the trials which I have already undergone & surmounted you would be astounded." His complaint is that his first officer had let him down. "The Mate (Mr. Ellis) is a Man that I cannot trust in any way therefore I have to act not only in my own Capacity but in his also." Davoll thought he had a mate "that can remember what is told him from one hour to another, but I am otherwise situated now & have been all the voyage." This is quite a change from his earlier positive assessments of his first-rate crew. Ellis's past experience suggested he "thoroughly knew his duty . . . but I am Sadly deceived & fairly disgusted with the Man, and the sooner he & I separates, the better." And soon they did part, as a vessel became available to take the mate and crew to Fremantle. To the captain this was an opportunity to "get rid of a great many incumbrances." He would stay behind with three men to wrap up the salvage.

Yet in the same letter he switches to a lighthearted tone as he describes to Libby his "Snug little House" on the beach at Port Gregory. "I have a little Office where I Lodge and do my writing Made of a Wooden Cistern sufficiently large for a place to sleep, with a little Table to write on—a Stand for wash Basin & Pitcher with plenty good water 6 feet from the door." He was as well taken care of as aboard ship. "I get my meals at the Tent with the rest of my officers. We live like fighting cocks on Fresh Beef, Mutton & fresh fish caught within 500 yards of my office—we have besides these luxuries all of the Ship's provisions to pitch into." The sand and dunes at Port Gregory even reminded him of Horseneck Beach back in Westport. Feeling "greatly blessed" for these comforts, he quickly adds, "although I am far from being where I want to be."

He was, in fact, conflicted about his situation and what to do when his responsibility to the *Iris* owners was fulfilled. "I am in duty bound to remain here & look after this horrid affair, therefore I am at a loss to say at what time I shall be released, but I

hope before long, for I want to come home to you very much."
At the same time, he considered staying for a year because "this
is a new Country & if a Man is any ways inclined to go ahead
there are flattering prospects for him to do so." He notes, "I
could pick up a few thousand if I had a little to start with." Still,
he doesn't know what that business would be: "I cannot as yet
say what I may do, but will either go into some business here
for the next year or come home the first opportunity." This of
course is not what Libby wanted to hear, so he wavers: "At all
events I think strong of coming direct home. Still can't posi-
tively say what I may do."[21]

What was this venture that promised such an extraordinary return on investment, and might it have been illegal or
just highly speculative? We don't know what he was thinking,
or who he had been in contact with besides the local magistrate, but it is tempting, in light of later events, to consider the
possibility of "blackbirding." This illegal practice involved the
recruitment and transportation of workers from Papua New
Guinea and other Pacific islands to Australia with assurances
of good jobs that turned out to be forced labor on Queensland
sugar plantations. Blackbirding was just beginning at this time
and proving very profitable for the carriers. Davoll was certainly considering some kind of lucrative venture, but there is
no proof that he was involved in blackbirding—although it is
an intriguing possibility.[22]

His indecision was likely a mix of his certainty that Libby
would be upset with him for even considering a year's extension
and his own need to salvage some financial compensation for the
Iris debacle. And he had heard that there was money to be made
in Australia, so why not make the best of being stranded there?
However, any venture he was considering would require some
capital, and he had no money to invest. His one-thirteenth lay
in the *Iris* voyage would be nearly worthless, and he had not yet
been paid for his portion of the oil or cargo salvaged. In any case,

the business opportunities proved ephemeral, and for reasons he never explained, Australia completely lost its allure: he had simply grown "sick and tired of this detestable country."

So he began making arrangements to return to New Bedford. After completing the disposal of the assets of the *Iris,* he and his remaining men boarded the *Rapid* and sailed to Fremantle. Hoping to return home as quickly as possible, he found a ship leaving for Singapore on December 20, but all he could do was post a letter to Libby, explaining that he had trouble coming up with the funds to return home, because he was unable to collect money due to him for the sale of items from the *Iris* wreck. While he waited, he met an American who owned a ship that would leave for Singapore in three weeks, and he wrote his wife that he would be home sometime in April. He was hoping that insurers or the *Iris*'s owners would pay at least half of his travel expenses.[23]

His time estimate was overly optimistic. In May Elizabeth received a letter from her brother-in-law Holder Russell, informing her that he had learned through a friend that Edward was aboard the *Wide Awake,* a clipper ship that plied the New York–to–Far East route in the 1850s. His expected date of arrival would be two months longer than expected. This had to be distressing news for Elizabeth, who needed him at home. And the delay only added to his financial woes. Time spent traveling aboard a ship that was not engaged in whaling was time wasted. Between his last successful whaling voyage and the start of his next one, it would be three years with little income. In May 1856, he returned home no closer to his goal of filling the hold with oil one last time and quitting the sea forever.[24]

CHAPTER 6

RECOVERY

W hen a whaling vessel returned to port after a typical voyage, there were a great many things to do. While agents took over much of the work at this point, the captain was involved in discussions with them about what worked on the cruise and what didn't, which crew members performed well and which to avoid, how the ship handled and whether any repairs were in order, and which grounds had been the most active with whales. There was mail collected from other ships to be delivered. And there was paperwork to be completed and the official dismissal of the crew with the collector of the port. Captain Davoll was very familiar with this routine.

This time it was different. He did not bring back the ship, did not have a crew to dismiss, and had no oil to unload or mail to deliver. He would also typically have spent time talking with owners or agents about his next trip, but this would be particularly difficult now. He had let down the *Iris* owners, and word certainly got out about the crew's displeasure. He was not officially blamed for the shipwreck, but a master's reputation with owners and agents, as well as with crew members whose share of the proceeds depended on a successful captain and a lucky ship, was vitally important. Davoll was not in disgrace, but his star had dimmed.

He decided not to seek employment with the *Iris*'s agent and primary owner, Edward C. Jones—or with anyone else from New Bedford. Instead, he went to Mattapoisett, a relatively small port seven miles to the east. In nineteenth-century whaling, Mattapoisett had a role similar to that of Westport, part of the New Bedford whaling district but also an independent port, with its own ships, agents, owners, and outfitters. As a young man Davoll had made his way from Westport to New Bedford for better career opportunities. Now his decision to move farther from the epicenter of the whaling industry suggests a degree of damage to his career that needed some time, and a successful voyage, to repair. It would be a "saving" voyage in more ways than one.

His family was also in need of repair. This was his second return as a married man, and one can imagine the combination of joy and awkwardness after two years' absence. There was also the possibility of pent-up anger: Why did you leave me for so long? Why didn't you write at every opportunity? This time there would be an added reason for tension, as he would have to explain the failed voyage. And now he would come home to a daughter that he had left a twelve-day-old infant and who was now a girl nearing two years of age who, except for a daguerreotype image, had never seen her father. This time, as well, he would become aware of family trouble: Elizabeth was not coping well with her life as a whaler's wife, and she was taking it out on little Carrie.

The family distress is evident from an extraordinary document that Edward Davoll composed for his wife, just as he was going back out to sea. It began as a set of instructions for handling financial matters: what to do when money came in and how to pay when a debt came due. He even wrote out two form letters for her to follow. This was essentially a written set of orders for Elizabeth, in the manner of the captain's orders to his crew in which he laid out the roles and responsibilities of each crew member; here he would do the same for his wife. He packaged these instructions in a three-by-five-inch notebook with a bright blue cover titled "Reference Book for Elizabeth S. Davoll by Edward S. Davoll, Aug 1856" and signed the letter "Your ob^t & humble Servant, E. S. Davoll"—both indications of the formality of the document.[1]

FIGURE 6. This family portrait shows Edward and Elizabeth Davoll with their daughter, Carrie, ca. 1856. When Captain Davoll returned from Australia in 1856, he had not seen his daughter in two years. Courtesy of the New Bedford Whaling Museum.

After the financial instructions, Edward entreats his wife to "be good to the child and not be passionate and abusive to her." Here we find what is most troubling about their situation: Libby has been whipping her daughter. Edward tries to give her advice, obviously based not on his very limited experience as a father but rather on his years as a captain. "Draw a straight line and keep her on it, which you can do if you adopt the right principle. Whipping will never do, and you must Stop it at once and use mild and gentle means which is for the best. . . . I truly believe that with these instructions you can do what is required."

It would be unfair given the sparse evidence to analyze the Davoll family's dysfunction, but a few things are clear. A mariner who genuinely misses his wife and essentially unknown daughter comes home after a humiliating shipwreck and financial loss to a woman who is lonely and, it appears, overly controlled by her often absent husband, and he finds that she has been taking out her unhappiness and frustration on their child. Carrie may have been hard to handle—we know very little about her—but it is evident that she was not the "model of perfection" that Davoll had envisioned after reading *Queechy*. Even a normally behaved child could be a challenge for a woman whose husband had been absent more often than not during six years of marriage. Children could be the saving grace of a whaling marriage, but as an insightful study of whaling families points out, "many other sea-wives found that maritime motherhood could be a both burdensome and compromised role." Elizabeth may have shared the feeling of another whaling wife who wrote to her absent husband, "I think it is rather lonesome to be shut up here day after day with three little children to take care of. I should be glad to know how you would like [it]."[2]

Davoll knows his wife is unhappy, not only because of his absences but also for her unsettled living arrangements. "I want you to have everything you need," he writes in the "Reference Book," "and to live where you are best suited whether in the Country or City, Board, Keep House or hang out just as you please." This is a familiar theme. They both wanted a home of their own, but Edward preferred that as he worked toward that goal they should continue to rent rooms in New Bedford rather than live in their hometown of Westport. Here he seems to be giving her a choice, but it was always he who decided.

Their situation was inherently difficult: a husband at sea and a wife essentially a single mother with no permanent home and not enough income to relieve the pressure. How much of this had to do with money? Despite the *Iris* disaster, the oil in the hold at the time of the shipwreck had been shipped to London, and the captain would get his share of the proceeds. Some money would come from insurance, possibly as much as $500. He also had income from oil that was his by virtue of his partial ownership of the *Cornelia*. Davoll claimed that with the sale of the oil from the *Cornelia*'s most recent voyage, he would have "nearly money enough out of my Share to Square all my debts, independent of what is due from the insurance offices, or Mr. Jones [the agent for the *Iris*]." If this is true, it would appear that he was not in terrible financial shape. His one-eighth ownership of the *Cornelia* was worth between $1,250 and $1,500, but he couldn't sell his shares without buying into another vessel or acquiring another asset, such as a house, because these shares were his pathway to the future and the only savings he had. And this was not enough for him to quit sailing yet or to buy the house they had been planning on for years. So now he was off to sea again, trying to improve his family's finances in order to transition to a job on land, while continuing the pattern that was tearing his family apart.[3]

The Mattapoisett agent Davoll turned to in this difficult time was Rogers L. Barstow. In addition to holding various political and civic positions, Barstow was a shipbuilder and a whaling owner-agent who controlled ten vessels, ranging in size from 70 to 295 tons. We don't know how Davoll and Barstow came to be acquainted, other than the fact that the fraternity of whaling captains and agents was relatively small and centered in New Bedford. Masters sometimes stayed with the same owner for multiple voyages, but it was more common for an owner and a master to join up for only a single voyage, so it was not unusual for Davoll to seek a different partnership. But in this situation, it wasn't simply a case of a captain shopping around for the best deal. Under these circumstances, Davoll was willing to settle for a smaller ship in a lesser port, and Barstow was willing to take a chance on a captain who had suffered a bit of bad luck.

Barstow offered Davoll the opportunity to invest in the *R. L. Barstow,* the vessel he would command, and Edward purchased four of the thirty-two shares. It was typical to spread the ownership among many investors as a hedge against shipwreck or a losing voyage. Offering a captain part-ownership of his vessel was also relatively common, as it provided an extra incentive for the captain to be aggressive in pursuing whales and to return with a full hold. So while not an unusual arrangement, it does indicate that Rogers Barstow was comfortable with a long-term relationship with Edward Davoll. And for the captain, it was a step toward his goal of becoming an investor in whaling voyages rather than master of a whaler constantly at sea.[4]

The *R. L. Barstow* was a 203-ton bark, built in Mattapoisett in 1851. Unlike the *Iris,* the *"RL"* was fairly new, but also relatively small—about the size of the *Cornelia* but considerably smaller than the 311-ton *Iris* (the average whaling vessel in this era was about 300 tons). A whaler of this size was usually intended for Atlantic voyages. The *RL* had gone on two previous Atlantic cruises, one of twenty-seven months that brought back 536 barrels of sperm oil and another of twenty-four months that returned with 409 barrels of sperm oil and 276 barrels of lesser-quality whale oil.[5] This cruise would also be in the Atlantic, which would be shorter than a Pacific or Indian Ocean voyage— suggesting another reason for Davoll's decision. He would not be away from his family for so long, although two years would still be a lengthy period for a family that evidently needed him.

The *RL* left port on August 19, 1856. Davoll had been home less than two months to mend his apparently shaky marriage and get to know his daughter. He departed a week after her second birthday. Weighing on his mind was the illness of his brother George, who was suffering from consumption. George died October 12, leaving a wife and at least one child. He was thirty years old.[6]

For the first part of the voyage Captain Davoll and his crew cruised the Atlantic whaling grounds. On February 15, 1857, he reported from St. Helena that the *RL* had taken 160 barrels of sperm oil and 10 barrels of whale oil. This tiny volcanic speck in the ocean is one of the most remote places on earth—the nearest mainland is twelve hundred miles away—which is why it had been selected by the British for Napoleon's exile after his defeat in 1815. Despite its reputation as a barren and desolate island, St. Helena was a popular stopping-off spot for whalers, visited by eleven hundred ships annually in the 1850s. In the opinion of George W. Kimball, the American consul, it was "one of the most beautiful in romantic wild scenery, and its 7000 inhabitants breathe the purest air and enjoy the finest climate in the world." The island had a safe and easily accessible harbor and an unlimited supply of fresh water. Thousands of visitors came each year to see the tomb and residence of Napoleon, although the remains of the emperor had been removed to France in 1840. Apparently, whalemen rarely tarried for the historical tour: the consul boasted that a ship could be resupplied in twenty-four hours and be on its way. But two *RL* crew members did remain behind: John Sherrard deserted, and Henry Augustus was discharged "on account of sickness brought on through drunkenness and debauchery." Losing Augustus was particularly inconvenient, as he owed the ship's store $74.78, considerably more than he had earned.[7]

For the next several months they cruised off the coast of Africa. The whaling was productive, but in May another man deserted at Little Fish Bay, and in July four men left the ship at Kabenda after stealing $1,000 worth of property. The captain paid "$5 for Negroes" to search for them. Captain Davoll's crew problems were making it increasingly difficult to maintain order and efficiency. In addition to discharges and desertions, he also had to deal with a man who several times was "sick and off duty with 'Venereal.'" These difficulties intensified the captain's growing distaste for whaling.[8]

By October 21 they had 500 barrels of sperm oil and 100 barrels of whale oil. In a letter to the *Whalemen's Shipping List,* the captain wrote that he was twenty days out of Little Fish Bay (present-day Namibia), where he had been recruiting men for a five-month cruise for sperm whales. In those twenty days he had added more barrels of sperm oil, but the last whale they took had been costly, resulting in a stove whaleboat and a serious injury to crew member Frank Perry. An ordinary seaman on the *RL*'s previous voyage, Perry was boatsteerer on the present one and apparently was hurt when his boat was smashed by the whale. He was injured so badly that he was unable to continue on the voyage and was discharged when the ship got to St. Paul de Loando (now Luanda, the capital of Angola).[9]

The next reported location, on March 20, 1858, was St. Helena, an indication that they were on their way home. They had 550 barrels of sperm oil and 100 of whale oil and would take a few more whales on their return. According to the captain, the whaling would have been much better had it not been for the third mate, Joseph Taber. In a letter to owner-agent Barstow, Davoll related in detail how Taber as boatheader (the man who delivered the killing blow to the whale with a lance) failed to take advantage of an opportunity in which "he could (if he had been half a man) killed half a dozen of them." The mate was, in the captain's view, "actually afraid of the fish." If, as Davoll claimed, Taber had not killed a single whale all voyage, he was certainly justified in blaming some of the poor results on the mate. It was too late for this voyage, but Davoll was putting his complaint in writing so that Taber would not be part of any Barstow-owned voyage in the future.[10]

The captain added a further, more general, point: "I want no more Portuguese Officers, Good Americans will answer my purpose." This suggests a strong prejudice, and there is ample evidence of Davoll's bias against foreigners, particularly people of color. If we look at his appraisal of specific whalemen, however, he is more evenhanded. When writing to Barstow about the mate who feared whales, Davoll provided a brief sketch of each crew member. Not surprisingly, Taber's was negative (to which he added "ugly sulky disposition"), as was that of the first mate, who was not officer material due to "habitual drunkenness." Yet the second mate was a "first rate sailor [and] tip top Officer," and other individuals were also highly rated—including some Portuguese.[11]

The *R. L. Barstow* arrived in New Bedford on August 30, 1858, with 680 barrels of sperm oil and 120 barrels of whale oil. For a relatively small vessel, out for two years in the Atlantic Ocean, this had to be considered a successful voyage. Although the 25 percent drop in the price of sperm oil since they had left port hurt Davoll's share, he likely earned about $1,800, plus his investor's share. The captain had brought in more oil than any previous cruise of the *RL,* and it would prove to be greater than any of its future voyages.[12]

Captain Davoll stayed home with his family for nine months. He had seen Carrie for only twelve days after she was born and for two months after he returned from Australia. Now she was four years old, a young girl that he still hardly knew, but this time he had the chance to interact with her on a broader level. There are no letters to tell us whether the beatings had stopped. Perhaps his extended stay brought some stability to the family.

Nine months was an unusually long time between voyages, especially for a man whose financial goals were far from being met. Certainly, he did not spend all his time getting reacquainted with family and friends. There were debts to settle and management of funds coming in from previous work (even the failed *Iris* voyage produced some income). There was whaling-industry information to learn and process, and there were discussions with agents to choose his next assignment. Based on the success of his recent voyage—and possibly still reticent to try New Bedford again—he decided to stay with Rogers Barstow and take command of the *RL* for another Atlantic cruise. Davoll still held four of the thirty-two shares in the vessel. Having completed a profitable voyage, his partial ownership had brought him income beyond what he earned as captain. He continued to see his future as an investor.

On May 20, 1859, the *R. L. Barstow* sailed out of New Bedford Harbor and into the open Atlantic. Just over a week later, about 250 miles northeast of Bermuda, disaster struck. The cooper, a man by the name of Allard (or Alland) Mahley, fell overboard. The seas were rough, and in the process of lowering a whaleboat to rescue him, the boat was "stove"—damaged enough to be unusable. The crew "then lowered another but could not save him. It was so rugged that he sank before we could get to him," the captain noted in the log. Two days later it was calm, and the men repaired the boat that had been smashed in the attempt to save the cooper. It appears that the inexperience or incompetence of the crew had contributed to the man's death. For the next two days Davoll ordered the boats lowered "to exercise the crew," apparently because they needed practice for normal whale chasing but also to be more competent the next time a similar emergency arose.[13]

A month later they had reached the western whaling grounds. Several whales were taken over the next three weeks, and the captain reported in a letter to the New Bedford whaling newspaper that he was now off Flores, the westernmost island in the Azorean archipelago, "with 100 bbls sperm oil, all well."[14] But all was not well at Flores. On August 3, the captain discovered that two of his crew members, E. Platt Welling, age twenty-one, and George H. Moon, seventeen, "had taken it into their heads to run away" and had already left the vessel. It would not have been hard to get replacement sailors among the Azoreans or Americans who had been discharged there and were looking for work. But this was desertion, a direct affront to his authority, and the captain would have none of it.

It was also more than a personal challenge. Because most seamen received a pay advance, usually amounting to one-quarter to one-third of projected earnings, the owners lost money if a man deserted before he had been productive enough to cover his advance. As the New Bedford agent Charles Morgan wrote to one of his captains, "I think you have a good crew but they are mostly all in debt to the ship from $70 to $100—so please take care they don't run away before you get some sperm oil."[15] Once a man had earned more than his advance, he was no longer in debt to the ship, and there are numerous instances of captains actually encouraging men to desert on the homeward leg in order to maximize profits. In this case, only a few weeks into the voyage, Davoll needed to recover the men both for his professional esteem as well as for the owners' profit.

The next day, Davoll took a boat into the village of Lagens, on the southeast coast of Flores, where he "had a Strict Search made for the deserters but found them not." He sent the boat back to the ship with a load of vegetables, chickens, and eggs and instructions to the first mate to take the *RL* out to cruise for whales while he stayed ashore to search for the men. The next morning he took a shore boat to Santa Cruz, about five miles to the north, and discovered that the runaways had been there, "purchased some bread & fled back into the Country." Santa Cruz was the administrative center for the island, and Davoll visited the consulate and left instructions that a search be conducted.

The following day a boat arrived from Santa Cruz carrying George Moon, the younger of the deserters. "He was very penitent and said he should never attempt to run away again," the captain wrote. "I forgave him & let him run at large Excepting nights when I locked him up. He staid in the house with me and was amply supplied with food." Davoll gave no explanation for his mild treatment of the deserter. We can only imagine that he took pity on a boy of seventeen who had been led astray.

By August 9, 1859, the captain was back on board the *RL*, which had taken a sixty-barrel sperm whale, and the crew was now boiling the blubber. (This proved to be a dangerous task for crew member Henry Lyon, who seriously injured his leg on the chime, or rim, of an oil cask.) Davoll got reports of other whalers, including the *Elizabeth* of his hometown of Westport. Although sharing the same name and home port of the vessel he had first gone to sea on, this was not the same *Elizabeth* (his former ship had been dismantled in 1842). This *Elizabeth*, a 270-ton bark, was holding six hundred barrels of sperm whale oil, most likely a reminder to Davoll that he had a long way to go to make a saving voyage.

The captain had not forgotten his other deserter. He took a boat into Santa Cruz and found that Welling had been captured but escaped, "taking to the Mountains." Davoll told the consul to offer a ten-dollar reward and to imprison the runaway next time. The captain noted that "Welling states that he had been abused with Knocks & Kicks which occasioned his deserting the vessel. All of which is as false as he has proved himself, to his duty."

After a week's cruise they pulled into Lagens again to "bargain for recruits" to replenish the crew. That day he received a letter from Santa Cruz informing him that "E. Platt Welling, Esq (our deserter) had been taken and was now in prison." Davoll took a boat to Santa Cruz and retrieved "Squire Welling." The references to "Esq" and "Squire" show the captain's disdain for the man, although there is no reference to his punishment. All Davoll wrote is "I think he will get better acquainted with whaling before he takes French leave again." "French leave" was the current term for an unauthorized absence.[16]

They continued to cruise around the Azorean Islands, including a "rugged run down the south side of Pico," with no additional oil. The only breaks were a visit with the bark *Solon* of

Westport and the bark *Sun* of Mattapoisett. The *Sun*'s captain, Daniel Flanders, came aboard the *RL* and stayed overnight, certainly a welcome opportunity for Davoll to speak freely with a whaleman who wasn't under his command. At the end of August he was laying off the coast of Fayal, "waiting to get a breeze" so that he could sail in close enough to take a boat ashore to discharge Franklin H. Fowler, "who has been raising blood from the Lungs for the last Eighteen days." The captain took Fowler in and, with health problems of his own, lingered at Fayal.

When he returned he noted in the ship's log, "From Sept 1st to 12th I was on shore out of health. Ship out cruising." His final log entry was on September 13. The next two pages of the log have been cut out, and then the log resumes on September 30, in distinctly different handwriting. Sometime between September 13 and 30, Captain Davoll had left the ship, relinquishing command to First Mate William H. Mitchell. The *RL* sailed to the Canary Islands and Cape Verde, crossed the equator into the South Atlantic, along the coast of Brazil, and returned to New Bedford eleven months after Mitchell took over. The bark never came back to pick up the former captain, nor is there any further mention of him in the ship's log.

At this point Captain Davoll disappeared from the public record. Even in an era of relatively poor communications, the location and status of the hundreds of whaling vessels scattered across the globe could be carefully traced in the pages of the *Whalemen's Shipping List*. Each week there was an updated table with the name of every active whaleship, its owner, captain, date of departure, last known location, and how much sperm oil, whale oil, and whale bone it had taken. Of course, its "current" location would be weeks out of date, as data slowly came in from letters and other ships in this worldwide network. But despite the time lag, it was surprisingly accurate. And for the period from September 1859 to August 1860, Captain Davoll's name is completely absent.

The reason for this silence is that Edward Davoll had been drawn into the transatlantic slave trade. And if the *Whalemen's Shipping List* was not keeping track of his whereabouts, the British consul in New York was.

British diplomatic personnel in New York diligently tracked suspected slavers. The consul, Edward M. Archibald, had been keeping an eye on a very large whaling ship called the *Atlantic,* which had been fitted out in New Bedford in 1859, under the command of Francis J. Silva. The owners were Abranches, Almeida & Co., known to be active in the slave trade. The *Atlantic* was a 699-ton former whaler originally from New London, Connecticut, but most recently a merchant vessel out of New York. On the surface the *Atlantic* looked like a legitimate whaler, and the owner helped his image by publicizing his intention to carry a load of corn, at cost, to help relieve famine in the Azores.[17] The ship raised suspicions because it was much larger than normal for a whaler, it carried seven whaleboats but listed a crew of only twenty-three men (more typical of vessel carrying three whaleboats), there was no first mate, one of the try-pots was cracked, and the lower hold was filled with casks of fresh water, whereas saltwater was usually used to keep casks from drying out. These were the sort of details that led federal authorities to suspect a false whaler. Yet when federal agents visited New Bedford in the summer of 1859 and detained the *Atlantic,* Mr. Abranches went there personally and "lulled the suspicions of the authorities." The ship then proceeded to the Azores, where Captain Silva, reportedly ill, turned over command to Edward Davoll.[18]

Silva's illness brought about a change in plans that was now to abandon the whaling voyage and take the ship to Boston. But according to Consul Archibald, "This was but a ruse [and] the ship should proceed to the African Coast for slaves." However, alerted by the British authorities, the U.S. consul at Fayal asked Davoll to transport twenty shipwrecked sailors to

Boston. The captain could not refuse (it was common practice to return American sailors by way of homebound whalers), and to claim he was not going to Boston would have made him more suspect. Thus, the consul was able to thwart a likely slaving venture.

The resulting voyage across the Atlantic involved no whaling—in fact, it was more of a passenger crossing, with forty-three men assigned by the consul and twenty-nine additional travelers in steerage (apparently in need of passage from the Azores to the United States). With ninety-two passengers in total, it was crowded. They left on November 3, and within a week crew member Ellis Busey was taken sick with back pain and "breaking out on the face and chest." The following week Hugh Biggins and James Kelly were vomiting and breaking out. The captain's comment about a fourth crew member was more dire: "Solomon Jones verry sick, passes nothing but blood from his bowels & raises fresh blood from his lungs or stomach. Think he can't live long."

This kind of outbreak, apparently contagious, was perilous on any voyage, but especially one with ninety-two people living in close quarters. None of the passengers became ill, and three of the sick crew members recovered, but on December 7 twenty-one-year-old Solomon Jones "breathed his last. Cause of death Dissenteria." Within two hours, they "committed his body to the deep, fearing to keep him on account of his stench. Previous to burial read the nineteenth chapter of Psalms."[19]

Davoll did not in fact go to Boston but sailed to New York, where the *Atlantic* sat for six months, as Consul Archibald kept watch. The ship was then fitted out for whaling. "The name of her master at the time of her clearance was Barker, an assumed name probably," according to Archibald, "but Davoll was the real commander."[20]

Several months later, the *Atlantic* ran aground in the Bahamas with a cargo of slaves aboard. In what Governor Bailey of the

Bahamas called a "daring outrage," the captain made his way to the Cay Lobos lighthouse, commandeered a boat, and somehow compelled two local schooners to transport the slaves to the Cay. The captain then forced one of the schooners to transport him to Nuevitas, Cuba, where he obtained a brig to convey the slaves to Cuba.

The report is believable, as it comes from the very reliable Consul Archibald. But was it Davoll who commanded the *Atlantic* from New York to Africa, then to the Bahamas, and finally delivered slaves to Cuba? Archibald claimed Davoll was in command when the *Atlantic* left New York. Governor Bailey named Davoll as the captain, but only in reference to the ship's departure from New York and not specifically when it was in the Bahamas. It was common for an American captain to cede control to a professional slaver on the coast of Africa and continue as a "passenger," making it difficult to prosecute. While it's possible that Davoll took the *Atlantic* out of New York in April 1860—perhaps to the Azores—he could not have been on board when the ship reached the Bahamas in December 1860, because during that interval he took command of the *Brutus* in New Bedford.[21]

CHAPTER 7

"WHAT'S IN THE WIND?"

When Captain Davoll returned to New Bedford in August 1860, a year after leaving command of the *R. L. Barstow* in the Azores, he began fitting out an unusually large whaling vessel. The *Brutus* was a 121-foot, 470-ton ship built in New York in 1845, originally intended for the Brazilian navy. In 1853 it was purchased by investors in Warren, Rhode Island, and made two Pacific whaling voyages in the 1850s. The ship's principal owner, R. B. Johnson, might have been in financial trouble. While whaling in the Okhotsk Sea in 1857, the *Brutus's* captain had salvaged oil, whalebone, anchors, sails, and other items of value from the wrecked bark *Newton* and never compensated the New Bedford owners for it. More recently, one of Johnson's whaling vessels, the *Dolphin,* had been wrecked on the coast of Patagonia, with the loss of the ship and eight hundred barrels of oil.[1]

Personal losses such as Johnson's, combined with a general downturn in the whaling business, a nationwide financial panic in 1857, and the glut of ships resulting from overbuilding for the California Gold Rush, put tremendous pressure on small whaling companies in minor ports, and sales of whaling ships were on the rise. Some of these sales were to well-financed New Yorkers with suspicious records.

The *Brutus* had been sold at auction in Warren on July 18, 1860, to buyers from New York, for $9,750. The whaling-industry newspaper reported, "She is to be withdrawn from the whaling business."[2] Less than a month later it was resold

FIGURE 7. The *Brutus* was fitted out in New Bedford by Captain Davoll in 1859, amid widespread suspicion that the whaling vessel was a slaver in disguise. Drawing by A. Lake. Courtesy of the New Bedford Whaling Museum.

to New Bedford wholesale liquor distributor Albert S. Bigelow and transferred to New Bedford, now "said to be for the whaling business." George Tripp was one of the crew that went to New York to transport the *Brutus* to New Bedford. "The *Brutus* was a fine, large, roomy ship, about the largest out of New Bedford in her time as a whaler. I worked on her as she fitted out on the north side of Propeller Wharf."[3]

Right from the start there was something fishy about the *Brutus*. The New York detour appears to have been due to the shadow ownership of Pierre L. Pearce, a shady ship chandler (a dealer in maritime outfitting goods) doing business at 27 South Street but implicated in numerous slave-trading voyages out of New York City. Pearce had connections to Spanish and Portuguese companies that were part of an Atlantic-wide network of financiers, slave procurers, agents, shippers, sea captains, and lawyers. Nor did Bigelow look particularly legitimate. The liquor dealer did not have a long history in whaling, nor was he likely to have had the means to be the sole owner of a whaling vessel. The quick resale to Bigelow suggested a sham ownership, financed by the slaving cartels of New York and Havana, and in fact was perfectly consistent with the common practice of placing ownership of a slaving vessel in the name of an American captain "or other obscure US citizens."[4] Thus, Bigelow was drawn into the web.

A New Bedford newspaper editorial—one year after the fact—summed up Bigelow's involvement nicely:

Ship "Brutus" ex Whaler, belonging to the port of Warren, R.I., arrived at this Port, coastwise from New York on August 14, 1860. She had been sold by her former owners to some one, and Bill of sale had been duly executed except that it contained no name as grantee. This omission was supplied by the insertion of that of "A. S. Bigelow," but the Bill of sale was not put on record. It was the current rumor at the time that the vessel had been purchased by parties in New York who proceeded to fit her for Whaling, but who, alarmed by the suspicions which attended the movements and fearing detention, concluded to sell, and that Mr. Bigelow purchased her at a great bargain on her arrival here. The new and sole owner proceeded to complete her outfit.[5]

Also involved was Andrew H. Potter, a New Bedford dry-goods merchant with a shop on South Water Street. Potter was working with Davoll and Bigelow to outfit the ship for a whaling voyage, specifically providing clothing to the crew. He was well known in New Bedford, with a prominent advertisement in every issue of the *Whalemen's Shipping List*. Many other people—carpenters, food and water provisioners, riggers, blacksmiths, caulkers, ropemakers—also supplied goods and services as the ship was prepared for sailing.

On August 21, the *Whalemen's Shipping List* reported that the *Brutus* was "seized by a U.S. officer on suspicion of being about to engage in the slave trade. She has been stripped of all her sails, and her outfit will be thoroughly examined for the purpose of ascertaining if there are any articles not usually put on board of whaleships."[6] The *Brutus* was not seized, however. Bigelow had offered to submit to a federal inspection, confident that no obvious violations would be detectable. Perhaps because of the owner's apparent sincerity, the inspection never took place.

The following week a Boston newspaper wrote of a Vigilance Committee that was "determined to put a stop to the slave trade from the eastern ports, and have so informed parties in New London, New Bedford, Fall River, Warren, and in other towns where suspicions have been entertained. They are promised support in all the places."[7] "What's up?" asked a New Bedford newspaper editorial as federal marshals visited town, "causing considerable fluttering in certain circles and quarters. What's in the wind? Are there any slavers fitting out at this Port?"[8] All this added up to an open secret that the owner and captain were preparing a slaver rather than a legitimate whaler.

Such news would have struck most New Bedford citizens as very troubling. This city with a deep Quaker heritage had been home to an active antislavery society since 1834 and maintained a reputation for relatively good race relations. Its role as an important hub of the Underground Railroad supported this reputation. A connection between its foremost maritime industry and the slave trade seemed unthinkable.

Despite five decades of ever-stricter laws against slaving, the 1850s were good years for the slave trade. The *New York Times* tallied 150 American slaving voyages from 1858 to 1861—the period of the *Brutus* excursion—with most of the slaves destined for Cuba. Sugar was king, and Cuba was supplying 30 percent of the world's demand. The insatiable taste for sugar was matched by the unquenchable need for slaves to work the expanding cane fields and to replace the slaves who were worked to death under brutal conditions. For much of the nineteenth century, the Atlantic slave trade had been concentrated on Brazil; now the focus was on Cuba. By 1850 there were nearly a half-million slaves on the island, most of them toiling on increasingly sophisticated sugar plantations.[9]

Regardless of the risks, the trade was too appealing for many Americans to pass up. As the *New York Times* put it, "perhaps no commerce was ever more profitable than the traffic in Africans."[10] Why take part in a whaling voyage with an average net return of 10 percent when a much shorter slaving voyage might yield ten times that amount?[11] While illegal—even *because* it was illegal—it was wildly lucrative, thriving on the indifference of most Americans, loads of international money, corrupt judges and port officials, and compromised enforcement. A running diplomatic war between the United States and Great Britain over the Royal Navy's right to search American commercial vessels rendered Britain's West African Squadron ineffective by allowing slavers to simply run up the American flag, knowing that the British navy could not touch them. Even John Quincy Adams, a dedicated foe to slavery, once stated that British interference in American commerce was worse than the slave trade![12] Politics, especially in a nation increasingly divided over slavery, made a simple matter of enforcing a federal law very complicated.

If Edward Davoll, or anyone else associated with the *Brutus,* was innocent of slave trading, this would have been a good time to distance himself from the impending voyage. But the captain and owner continued to play a cat-and-mouse game with the authorities (Davoll's name was not on the official registry; listed instead was John Hursell, the captain who had ferried the ship from New York to New Bedford). Bigelow was in a rush to clear the port but held back when informed by the pilot boat that the U.S. revenue cutter *Harriet Lane* was cruising outside the harbor.[13] This served only to confirm the suspicions of the citizens of New Bedford—the "plain talk about the matter" bruited about the city. To allay such concerns, Bigelow had offered to allow a government inspection, but hearing that the *Harriet Lane* had left the area, he quickly got local clearance and made arrangements for a tug to tow the *Brutus* out of the harbor, and on August 28 Captain Davoll set sail for the open Atlantic. Second in command was First Mate William H. Jackson of Portsmouth, Rhode Island. Most of the twenty-four crew members believed that the voyage would adhere to its stated goal of whaling in the Atlantic and Indian Oceans.[14]

The captain and owner had cleverly avoided a government inspection, but in fact an examination would have done little good. Despite grave misgivings, the *Brutus* looked enough like an ordinary whaler on a legitimate voyage to prove definitively that it was anything else. The New York slave-trade agents had figured out that whalers were easily passed through standard port inspections. A slave ship needed ample space below deck to accommodate hundreds of Africans: a whaler had a huge hold. A slaver needed some means to cook food for its human cargo: a whaler had a tryworks—the boiler used to render whale blubber into oil, which was easily adapted for cooking rice or porridge. A slaving voyage required an extraordinary amount of fresh water: a whale ship had a large supply of barrels that could be used for water rather than oil. A customs inspector or naval officer could examine this ship from stem to stern and find nothing that proved it to be a slaver. In this age of extraordinarily fast clipper ships and steam-powered vessels, a slow but artfully disguised whaling ship proved to be a very practical and efficient slaver.

The *Brutus* made for the Azores. At Flores the ship "laid off and on" while Davoll was rowed to shore, with his trunks. After a wait of one or two hours, the ship sailed away under the command of Mate Jackson. As suspected, the ship proceeded to the African coast, where a Spanish captain and "surgeon" came aboard. It was at this point that the crew members who thought they had shipped for a legitimate whaling voyage were informed that they were on a slaver. Some of the crew had known in advance what the object of the voyage was; these were professional mariners who were happy to take the high wages for working in the trade. Those who objected faced a stark choice: to be left on the coast of Africa to fend for themselves or to remain on the ship and do as ordered. Two of the men, Second Mate Charles R. Chase, of New York, and Steward Charles Pierce, of Calais, Maine, chose to take their chances in Africa; the rest stayed with the ship.[15]

Mate Jackson navigated, but the Spanish captain was in charge of the slaving operation, apparently experienced in such matters. The *Brutus* proceeded to the mouth of the Congo River, met with slave traders, and arranged for the purchase of a large number of African men, women, and children. After this initial contact had been made, the *Brutus* sailed out to sea and gave the appearance of whaling for several weeks. This was a ruse: the men "were laying round the decks most of the time." So good was the disguise that an encounter with the U.S.

Navy sloop of war *Mohican* near the mouth of the Congo River proved no threat to the slavers. When asked what he was doing in the vicinity, Jackson claimed he was cruising for humpback whales in order to train his greenhands. The naval officers examined the ship's papers, "looked into the hold, but didn't go down," and declared that the whaler was clean.[16]

Then, on an agreed-upon date, February 14, 1861, the *Brutus* returned to the African coast for its human cargo. Seven hundred slaves were to be brought to the ship lying at anchor at Devil's Point. During the process of ferrying them, fifty of the captives drowned, and fifty were left behind. Six hundred slaves were loaded onto the ship between eight in the morning and five in the afternoon, along with beans, corn, beef, pigs, and goats. With slaves on board, the "whaler" was now a slaver, and in his haste to avoid another encounter with the U.S. Navy, the mate discarded the anchor and chain and quickly sailed off. The captive men were crammed into the hold, with no shackles; the women and children were kept on deck. The conditions, especially below deck, were appalling: one hundred slaves died on the suffocating passage across the Atlantic and were discarded overboard. This was no surprise to the slavers: they expected a 15 percent loss of life. To men who would ship human beings as if they were cattle, this was simply "spoilage," already factored into the financial calculation.[17]

It typically took about six weeks to navigate the Middle Passage across the Atlantic to the West Indies.[18] As the *Brutus* approached Cuba, a Spanish pilot came on board to guide them in. The ship was run aground off the southeast coast of the island, about three miles from Santiago. Three boats came out from shore, and along with two whaleboats from the *Brutus* the crew landed the five hundred Africans who had survived the voyage.[19]

The slaves and crew were transported in carts six miles into the country, to a plantation where they were lodged in a sugar house, crew on the upper level and slaves below. The *Brutus* was left in the hands of "some Spaniards" and, depending on the source, was either burned, left to break up in the surf, or sold. (It is a measure of the outlandish profitability of the slave trade that the slaving vessel could be abandoned with little effect on the bottom line.) The crew were kept in the sugar house for eighteen days. One member, Frederick Standish (from Foxboro, Massachusetts), died and was buried in Cuba. Mate William Jackson, who had been a willing participant from the start, along with blacksmith Thomas Jeffrey stayed in Cuba, apparently to continue in the slaving business. The rest of the crew were put on a fishing smack and taken to Key West and from there made it back to their respective homes.

The sailors were well paid for their participation. The lowliest foremast hands, who might have earned $100 for a two-year whaling cruise, received $500 for a slaving voyage of less than a year. There were risks—of slave revolt, yellow fever—in addition to the fact that what they were doing was illegal. But there were men willing to do it, out of greed and moral indifference. Some had been tricked into it and went along because there was no other viable choice. Most would never do it again, but they kept their mouths shut—and kept the money.

This was not the case for two brave first-time sailors from Belchertown, Massachusetts. Milo Robbins and Jerome Colburn, both in their late teens, had decided to try whaling in 1860 and met with a recruiter on Commercial Street in Boston, who sent them to New Bedford. There they were provided at the store of A. H. Potter with "three pairs pants, four shirts and drawers, two hats, pipes, tobacco, beds and blankets." They lodged at the boardinghouse of George Long until the day their ship hurriedly left the harbor. Once at sea the boys were puzzled by the captain's departure at Flores and finally learned the true purpose of the voyage off the coast of Africa. Offered the choice of being left on the Congo coast or acquiescing in the slaving mission, both young men opted to continue the voyage.

However, they did not remain silent when they finally returned to Belchertown. It is unclear if Colburn testified in court, but the seventeen-year-old did tell his story to newspapers, relating the basic facts of a supposed whaling voyage that delivered five hundred slaves to Cuba. Robbins told a lot more, providing detailed court testimony that recounted ("in a plain, straightforward manner, which bore strong evidence of its truth") the boarding of the slaves at Devil's Point (near Cabinda in present-day Angola), the drownings, the deaths from disease and suffocation during the passage to Cuba, the landing and sale of the slaves, and his own eventual delivery to Florida. He also confirmed that Captain Davoll left the ship in the Azores and that the first mate took command. Robbins paid a price for his courage: he spent nine months in a Boston jail as a witness. He was not under arrest, but witnesses who lacked the means to pay for lodging were put up at the jail and compensated one dollar per day for their trouble. [20]

Based on this testimony, Deputy U.S. Marshal S. H. Bicknell traveled from Boston to New Bedford on August 8, 1861, with warrants for the arrest of the owner, Albert Bigelow, and outfitter, Andrew Potter. Early the next morning Bicknell gained the cooperation of the city marshal, Elias Terry, and together they went to Bigelow's store on South Front Street, where the merchant complied with the warrant. Then, Bigelow in tow, the two officers proceeded to South Water Street to confront Potter at his dry-goods store. He also cooperated, and by midday the marshal, Bigelow, and Potter were on the train to Boston. The two men were charged with preparing the *Brutus* for "the trade and business of procuring Negroes, mulattoes, and persons of color from . . . the continent of Africa to be transported to . . . the island of Cuba, to be held, sold, and otherwise disposed of as slaves." [21]

Pierre Pearce, the wily New York slave trader, who was currently facing a slaving charge in New York, was summonsed to Boston. His lawyer tried for a reduction of bail from $10,000 to $5,000. It soon became clear why: once Pearce was freed, he quickly left the country.[22] In late August 1861, almost exactly one year since the *Brutus* had left port, Bigelow and Potter were examined by a U.S. commissioner. Potter was discharged due to lack of evidence. While it was clear that he had supplied the crew with clothing and had paid for their lodging at Long's boardinghouse, it would have been difficult to prove Potter's knowing involvement in slaving—he could have sworn that he had innocently fitted out a legitimate whaler, as he had done many times before. And indeed, the *Brutus* looked very much like an authentic whaler. The court "considered the evidence insufficient that [Potter] was cognizant of the business in which the ship was about to engage, that he furnished the usual outfits, and that in line with his business."[23]

Not so for Bigelow who, the commissioner ruled, "knew the character of the voyage." C. B. Fessenden, the collector of the Port of New Bedford, testified that Bigelow had signed all the official papers—registry, bond for seamen, shipping articles, manifest—that established his clear ownership of the *Brutus,* making it difficult for him to deny knowledge of the voyage's purpose. Earlier he had tried to invalidate his ownership: just days after the *Brutus* sailed, he executed a power of attorney to Pierre Pearce, who a week later sold the ship to William H. Cowdrey of New York. This ploy, so commonly used in the history of American involvement in the slave trade, fooled no one. With Bigelow's bail set at $10,000, the grand jury of the U.S. District Court of Boston "returned a true bill against Albert S. Bigelow for fitting out the ship 'Brutus' for the Slave Trade."[24]

What did the citizens of New Bedford think of this engagement in slave trading from their port? A newspaper editorial at the time of Bigelow's indictment suggests that public opinion doubted his innocence, that the *Brutus* had been transferred to their port to escape prosecution in New York, and that the good people of the city had suspected it all along. "Before sailing of the *Brutus,* other ships, the *Memphis, Atlantic, Comora, Tahmaroo,* had left this Port under circumstances more or less suspicious—in fact, our Community though destitute of any positive knowledge on the subject to warrant their interference, entertained but little doubt that all these vessels intended to engage in the Slave Trade. . . . Of the *Brutus* there was less doubt still," the editorial continued, "and the rumor in reference to her having landed a cargo of slaves confirmed the opinion of the illicit character of her voyage." That generally held suspicion, of course, had not led to action at the time, but now "we do heartily hope that the guilty may be detected and punished, and not by an insignificant mullet—for in no other way can these nefarious traffics be terminated."[25]

This accounts for most of the principal players in the outfitting of the slaver, but where was Edward Davoll while all this was going on? He had left the *Brutus* sometime late in September 1860 at Flores. No doubt he claimed illness, just as he had when he left the *R. L. Barstow* in the Azores in 1859. The public knew nothing about the *Brutus* at this point, but the captain had to act carefully because of the suspicion aroused when the ship was being outfitted. Presumably, he returned to his family in New Bedford within a month or two, at which point he needed to get back to work, both for the income and to maintain the appearance of a legitimate whaling master. In April 1861 he took command of the small whaling schooner *Palmyra,* managed by A. H. Potter, the dry-goods merchant who had been one of the outfitters of the *Brutus.*

CHAPTER 8

EVASION

~~~

The 100-ton schooner *Palmyra* was small for a whaler, even smaller than the two Westport brigs that Davoll had sailed on in his earliest days of whaling. Following the industry trend of ever-larger vessels and increasingly longer voyages, Davoll had moved up to the 216-ton bark *Cornelia* and then the *Iris* at 311 tons. The *R. L. Barstow* was smaller but fit the captain's needs after the debacle in Australia. His next ship was by far the largest, the 470-ton full-rigged three-masted *Brutus,* which, as became evident, was chosen for its capacity for a cargo of slaves rather than for whale oil.

The little schooner, built in Plymouth in 1839, had begun whaling at Nantucket before being transferred to Mattapoisett in 1856. In October 1860, just two months after the *Brutus* sailed, the *Palmyra* returned from a cruise in the Atlantic and was moved to New Bedford under the ownership of Andrew H. Potter (along with two partners in his dry-goods shop) and Edward Davoll. The captain owned half the shares. Where he got the roughly $1,500 to buy the shares is unknown. Perhaps he had already been paid for his part in the slaving voyage. Payment usually came after the delivery of the slaves, which had not yet occurred at this point, but because his part in the deal called for his dropping out before any slaves were purchased, he might have been paid in advance.[1]

Not only was the *Palmyra* undersized for a captain who was looking to make one last big haul that would allow him to retire, but as a schooner it was poorly rigged for whaling.

Most whalers—brigs, barks, and ships—had square sails (the kind seen now on tall ships). Schooners had "fore and aft" sails (the shape most often associated with modern sailboats), with booms that swung far to either side of the vessel. The swinging boom often got in the way when a whale was being processed, so most owners and captains preferred square-riggers.[2]

So why would Davoll go to sea on a small, inappropriately rigged whaler? One reason is that it was guaranteed to stay in the Atlantic (the *Palmyra* had never whaled anywhere else), so he wouldn't be too far from home. Another is that its half owner was A. H. Potter (who like Davoll was originally from Westport). Potter had been a major outfitter of the *Brutus* and, along with the sham owner, Bigelow, had been arrested. Although discharged by the grand jury, Potter—like Davoll—was under a cloud of suspicion. Other agents and owners were likely to remain wary of the captain.

The overriding reason for his choice of vessel seems to be that Davoll was on edge about his recent voyage. He had returned to New Bedford where people were wondering about the outcome of the *Brutus* voyage. Why had the captain left the ship? Had it gone to Africa for slaves? Even Davoll didn't know the actual outcome, but he knew his own part. He needed to get to sea—both to earn a living and, more important, to lay low for a while. We don't know what he was thinking at this point because, as one might expect, his letters never mention anything about slaving. But we can surmise that he needed to buy time for it to blow over and for suspicion to abate. If all went well, the *Brutus* would be burned (or sold in Cuba with a name change), and the crew, following the typical pattern, would claim that they had been shipwrecked and make their way back to the United States. The sailors would be pleased with their pay and would say nothing about how they got it. This is how so many slaving voyages had gone for decades, and it would not have been foolish to expect that the *Brutus* affair would end similarly.

Complicating matters was the fact that on April 12, 1861, as the *Palmyra* was being readied, the Civil War had begun with the attack on Fort Sumter, ushering in a time of fear and uncertainty. Mariners would still go to sea, but whaling would get more expensive, as insurance rates soared. And even though the Confederate navy was no match for the Union navy, Northern shipping and whaling, with their slow and usually unarmed ships, became targets for privateers and commerce raiders. Whaling continued: the Union still needed whale oil and baleen, maybe more than ever, but it was an uneasy time to be on the ocean. The only advantage was that men at sea were exempt from the Massachusetts draft, and many preferred the risk of capture by a privateer to the dangers faced by common army soldiers.

The *Palmyra* left New Bedford on April 24, 1861. Davoll had only fifteen men in the crew and just two whaleboats. This was low-budget whaling, not the high-potential cruise he was used to—or needed for retirement. But it kept him away from New Bedford. This does not mean that he was uninterested in bringing in whales. In several pages of the logbook he had written:

> A Standing Bounty for the Voyage
> Look Sharp!! Look Sharp Aloft!!!

In a directive to the crew he was more specific: "You who want money will please bear in mind that a standing Bounty of ten dollars for every one hundred barrels of Sp oil stowed down on the voyage will be rewarded to the man who first Sings out for the whales & reports the same to the deck, and in same proportion for smaller quantities." The captain might have ulterior motives for being at sea, but this was still a whaling voyage.[3]

There is no information about the early part of the cruise (the partial log of the *Palmyra* starts in August), but there are indications that the whaling in the Azorean grounds had not been very successful. Davoll did have some good financial news to relay to his wife, however. The proceeds of the voyage of the *R. L. Barstow* in 1859—the one he left abruptly in the Azores—had been settled, and his share came to more than $1,300. So while the current cruise had less potential than he was accustomed to, he did have money coming in from a previous voyage. Apparently, Libby had written recently with news that she had been ill since he left but was improving; in response he was "hoping you will regain your health soon & Eat Hearty, Grow fat and Saucy." She had also brought up the matter of her residence, expressing a wish to move from their rented rooms in New Bedford but asking for his opinion. He advised her to stay. "We have a good tenement in a good locality." After eleven years of marriage, they still had no place of their own.[4]

By mid-August 1861 the *Palmyra* had sailed away from the Azores, toward the southwest. There were no whales and little to note except meeting up in mid-Atlantic with the whaling brig *Kate Cory* from Westport. Davoll and Captain Stephen Flanders exchanged information about how much oil each had taken, and it is tempting to wonder if they discussed the risks of whaling during the Civil War. Captain Flanders would directly face that danger when the *Kate Cory* was captured and burned by the Confederate commerce raider *Alabama* in April 1863.[5]

As he crossed toward Bermuda, Davoll had a lot on his mind. When would he see and capture a whale? Were there any Confederate privateers in the area to overtake and burn his schooner? What did anyone know about the *Brutus*? Could he resume his career without accusations of slave trading? Was retirement even possible now? All this stress seems to have brought him to the breaking point in early September, in a brutal confrontation with one of his crew.

At three o'clock in the morning of September 4, 1861, far from shore in the mid-Atlantic, Captain Davoll left his cabin for a walk on the deck of the *Palmyra*. There he found William Robinson, a young boatsteerer who had fallen asleep on the mid-to-four watch. When Robinson denied he had been sleeping, the captain struck him and called the first and second mates to bring rope to tie the young man in the rigging. Davoll then flogged the boatsteerer. The only description of the incident is in the ship's log kept by Davoll and is worth reading in its entirety.

At 3 A.M. I went on deck & caught Wm Robinson (Boatsteerer) asleep & when I gave him a scolding for it he denied being asleep & undertook to make me believe my Eyes deceived me. I took hold of him, when he in great fury Said let go of me, but I let go when I got ready [and] told him to get into the Cabin. He did so & I followed him, called the Mate & Second Mate & told them to get some spun yarn [rope] for seizing him into the rigging when he said there was not men Enough in the vessel to do it & began to make use of his insolence. I told him to be quiet but he would not. I then took hold of him again, when he said don't you Strike me, D—n you don't you Strike me, but I did strike him & he undertook to return the blow but I kept him at bay. When I released him he ran on deck Swearing he would Kill the first man that layed hands on him. Same drawing a knife. I told the officers to Seize him & tie him up at once. He resisted them with all in his power. Still not making any use of a Knife. With my assistance we managed to get him Securely tied. I then talked to him very cooly & asked him if he was not in the rigging! Etc., Etc. I also told him that I should Flog him & made preparations for the purpose, by making a cat of Spun yarn. When I was all ready I told him that I should take it Easy but for choice I would much rather be the one to receive the blows than receive [he means give] them & then I commenced gave him three blows only when he begged like a dog. I then talked to him for awhile & found him penitent. He promised to do in future the best he knew, therefore he was released. Latter part [of the day] strong breezes & Squally.[6]

Flogging was one of the most severe punishments in the maritime services. The victim was tied in the rigging and beaten on the back with a "cat" (cat-o'-nine-tails), a whip made of multiple strands of rope or "spun yarn." The goal was to lacerate the skin, cause intense suffering, and humiliate the victim, as well as to send a clear message to crewmates who were forced to observe the punishment. The humiliation was particularly important: note how Davoll was satisfied when his victim "begged like a dog." Opponents to the practice noted that flogging "carried the stigma of slavery."[7]

Punishment by flogging had been banned by the U.S. Navy in 1850, and the prohibition extended to commercial vessels as well, although not everyone agreed with the ban. Even the rather staid *Whalemen's Shipping List* lamented the law against flogging with an article on the increase in desertions in the whaling fleet. "Discipline has already received a death-blow at the hands of the land-lubber legislators and judges who have meddled, in a spirit of false philanthropy with things they did not understand." The article went on to opine that "since the abolition of flogging, our Navy is on the wane."[8] Captains opposed laws that limited their means of discipline, especially one that they believed was effective. Other mariners felt that flogging was never justified, "for God never made one man, however high that man's station is, to have a brother man tied up in the rigging, and flogged with a stiff piece of rope. There is no reason, no consistency, no humanity, no love to God or man in such a case."[9]

Why would the captain enter this incriminating description of flogging into the ship's log? Most likely, he wanted his side of the story to be documented in case he was later accused of brutality. Apparently, he thought he was justified and that he had in fact been "easy" on the boatsteerer by applying only

FIGURE 8. Flogging was the most severe punishment meted out by captains. Crew members were forced to watch, as a deterrent to disobedience. Flogging was outlawed by the U.S. Navy and maritime service in 1850, so Davoll's flogging of his subordinate in 1860 was illegal. *A Picture for Philanthropists,* Art and Picture Collection, New York Public Library, New York Public Library Digital Collections. http://digitalcollections.nypl.org/items/510d47e1-1d3f-a3d9-e040-e00a18064a99.

three stripes. Yet the punishment does appear extreme, especially with no indication that Robinson had done this before. And falling asleep, while serious and worthy of a reprimand, was hardly in the category of mutiny or desertion. We remember how moderate Davoll had been with his two deserters aboard the *R. L. Barstow,* certainly a worse transgression than Robinson's. His own orders to the crew (from a previous voyage) instructed his officers to use nonviolent means whenever possible. This also brings to mind that he had implored his wife not to beat their child: gentler methods always work best. Certainly, Davoll was not shy about enforcing discipline aboard ship—a captain had to—but he seems to have gone well beyond his usual strictness. A man will do unusual things when under severe stress; Davoll was understandably apprehensive about what was known about the *Brutus* voyage and whether his life was about to unravel.

This would be a good time to review what kind of captain Davoll had become. He knew whaling very well, from first-hand experience as he worked his way up. He appears to have been insecure at first—certain that others resented his rise through the ranks and talking behind his back, but time took care of that. There are indications that he was strict, but not a tyrant. He often had good things to report about young sailors ("an active and smart lad, quick to learn . . . will in time make a tip top man") and even had praise for specific Azorean and Cape Verdean seamen that he generally disparaged. Back when he was master of the *Cornelia,* he had written a long letter to Libby in defense of ordinary sailors, ranting how badly they were taken advantage of by owners, agents, outfitters, and other "land sharks." Some of his best moments on board were spent "smoking & chewing tobacco, telling stories with the mates and Boatsteerers" in the evenings. He doesn't appear to be the kind of martinet who would resort to the lash.[10]

On the other hand, on the first *R. L. Barstow* voyage, Davoll had been "under the necessity of inflicting upon [boatsteerer Joseph B. Smith] severe punishment." We don't know if it involved flogging, but in any case it was harsh. Nor do we know the offense, although the captain blamed the first and third mates for not keeping Smith under control. Otherwise, Davoll considered him "a tip top man in every respect," who would not have been punished "had the man been kept at a distance from" the two inept officers. We might consider this poor management on the part of the captain, whose lack of control over two of his mates forced him to severely punish a good man.[11]

In flogging Robinson, Davoll had clearly overstepped his personal ethics as well as the law, and not over desertion or mutiny but for sleeping on watch and back talk. It's true that the captain could not be casual about sleeping on watch; as one whaling master had advised a promising sailor, "Discharge any officer who allows himself habitually to sleep on his watch." But note that the punishment was discharge, not flogging, and the offense had to be habitual, not once. The stress of Davoll's situation had clouded his judgment.[12]

On the day after the punishment, the crew captured three whales. Two were small, yielding only twelve and fifteen barrels, while the third produced a healthy sixty barrels. But their luck didn't hold. The captain's log entries often ended with "Looking sharp for whales" or "Looking sharp for sperm fellow." Obviously distressed with no whales to process into oil, he ended one entry with "Looking sharp for something to create a grease spot." On October 2 they sighted but couldn't capture four sperm whales. "When shall we meet again," the captain wondered.[13]

Then on October 17 they spotted a sperm whale that the captain estimated at one hundred barrels—exactly what they desperately needed. The schooner "gullied [frightened] the whale by running over him." The two whaleboats were quickly lowered in pursuit. One boat got close: "Shot one bomb lance into him, but not to hurt him." Pulled by the struck whale, the whaleboat went out of sight of the schooner for more than an hour, and the crew were forced to cut the line. This near miss was the most frustrating kind of loss. Like many log keepers, Davoll used whale stamps to indicate a whale caught (with the number of barrels of oil produced) or a whale lost. For this particular whale he added the caption "Went to the Devil."[14]

FIGURE 9. Logbook whale stamps recorded whales captured or lost. Having harpooned but lost a large whale, Captain Davoll added the caption "Went to the Devil." Log of the schooner *Palmyra*, courtesy of the New Bedford Whaling Museum.

October storms didn't help. "A tremendous sea on," Davoll
noted. "Stove starboard boat. Had decks full of water, etc, etc."
Despite less oil than hoped for, the captain was "work[ing]
towards home," but first they would make their way to Bermuda.
They sighted the island on November 7, 1861. That day there was
another stove whaleboat—this time not from a storm but by the
boat-lowering crane (or davit) giving way, thus adding equipment failure to the litany of problems encountered on the voyage. On Sunday, November 10, the captain spotted the Bermuda
lighthouse and drew a sketch of it in the logbook.[15]

FIGURE 10. Captain Davoll must have been relieved when he arrived at Bermuda during
the Civil War without encountering any Confederate raiders. He sketched this drawing
of the Bermuda lighthouse in his logbook. Log of the *Palmyra*, courtesy of the New
Bedford Whaling Museum.

The last log entry was on Monday, November 11: "At 6 P.M.
took a Pilot on board who states that war between the Northern
& Southern states still Exists & that but a few days ago two
Privateer Steamers were here." This undoubtedly added to
Davoll's relief in having reached Bermuda without being cap-
tured by a Confederate ship. The captain also noted that they
had "passed a Bark (American) laying at anchor outside the
Entrance of the harbor, who put in, in distress, leaking badly.
Cargo Sugar." Any resemblance to his situation would have been
lost on the captain: like this ship, he was an American in distress,

and the cargo of sugar was probably produced by slaves who had been transported from Africa to Cuba by slave traders.

A few days after arrival, the *Palmyra* tied up to a British brig, the *Princess Royal,* and began to transfer oil to be sent home. The keeper of the log (most likely the first mate, Charles Shaw) noted on November 16 that the cook, Robert Williams, had gone ashore without permission. That was just the beginning. On the twenty-first the keeper wrote: "At 8 A.M. David Mendall (the 2nd officer) refused to do any more duty in the presence of Captain Davoll. Took his things and went on board the *Princess Royal*. At 10 Wm Robinson (Boatsteerer) went on shore." Robinson was the man that Davoll had flogged in September.

The following day, after a fourth man had joined the others, the captain ordered that no boats could leave the schooner without his consent. It did no good: over the next two days, six more men stole away. Davoll ordered the mate to go ashore, find the men, and force them to return immediately. All refused. The deserters now represented two-thirds of the total crew. The log ends the following day—a suggestion that the mate keeping the log had gone to join the others.[16]

No existing logs or letters explain why the captain had lost control of his crew, but two factors seem likely. His flogging of the boatsteerer (and Robinson's early departure) suggests that the illegal punishment had turned the men against the captain. They may also have been dismayed that Davoll was preparing the *Palmyra* to winter over in Bermuda, when the plan had been to return to their home port.

On the same day that the second mate and boatsteerer left the ship, Davoll wrote to Libby without mentioning the problems with his crew but did relate that he was sending thirty-five casks of sperm oil to New York and would like to be on that ship, but felt he must stay with the *Palmyra* to "see her perfectly secured for the winter." He promised to be home after attending to the vessel. He added that he considered sending for her, but, he claimed, the winter gales would be too rough for her—and might delay his own passage home. Plus, there were Confederate privateers in the waters off Bermuda. He seemed to have plenty of reasons to keep him from returning.[17]

The fear of Confederate privateers was real. During the Civil War, despite Britain's proclamation of neutrality, Bermudians had distinct Southern sympathies. As a Bermuda historian put it, "Bermuda's bonds with the South, a general dislike of Yankees and the proliferation of Southern ships, Southern sailors and Southern agents in St. Georges all served to influence public opinion on the Island."[18] As a New England Yankee, Davoll could not have felt entirely comfortable, but he stayed on.

In his letter to Libby, he omitted the real cause of his delay at Bermuda. Sometime during the voyage, Davoll had heard that the *Brutus* affair had been exposed. He received confirmation in a letter from a New Bedford friend named Gifford who related the news that another New Bedford whaling master, Samuel Skinner, had been arrested, tried in Boston District Court, and convicted in November 1861 of fitting out the *Margaret Scott* for the slave trade. He had been sentenced to five years in the Taunton jail and fined $1,000. Skinner's story will be related later; for now, what is important is the effect of his conviction on Davoll.

If Edward Davoll had not grasped the similarity to his own situation, his friend's letter had more explicit news. "I suppose you have heard of Potter & Biglow [sic] being arrested some time ago. Potter is cleared Biglow is under one thousand dollar bond I think he will have his trial the last of this month." Bigelow looked "care worn" and was "sorry he had anything to do with that fitting business." Gifford had also spoken with another New Bedford captain, Shubael F. Brayton, who was certain that Bigelow was waiting for Davoll to return as a witness. Brayton's advice was for Davoll to stay away until the trial was over. "I have not heard [anyone] else say anything about the matter," his friend concluded, "but I guess that will all be settled before Spring, and I will write you [with] the full particulars of the trial."[19]

So now the news of the true mission of the *Brutus* was public, Bigelow was on trial, and Davoll was advised to stay away as long as possible. He lingered at Bermuda throughout the winter and spring. Despite the beauty and fine weather of Bermuda, his situation was grim: he was away from his family, not engaged in whaling, living in a "den of secessionists," and facing federal prosecution in Massachusetts. Then in June 1862, either hoping that Bigelow's conviction would somehow not affect him or simply realizing that he could hide no longer, he made the decision to return to his family in New Bedford and face the consequences.

He arrived home sometime during the fourth week of June by way of another ship (the *Palmyra* would not return until August 12). By now everyone in New Bedford knew all about the voyage of the sham whaler *Brutus*. Captain Davoll could not have been surprised when, on June 26, a federal marshal paid a visit.

CHAPTER 9

THE CASE AGAINST
CAPTAIN DAVOLL

O n July 1, 1862, Edward Davoll received some unwelcome publicity in New Bedford's *Whalemen's Shipping List:* "On Thursday last [June 26], Capt. Edward S. Davoll, of this city, was arrested by U.S. Marshal Cobb, and taken to Boston before U.S. Commissioner Merwin, on a charge of taking to sea the ship *Brutus,* for the purpose of procuring a cargo of slaves. On motion of the counsel for the defence [*sic*], a continuance was granted to the 1st of September, the defendant giving bonds in the sum of $2,500."[1]

Now in the first full year of the Civil War, the slave trade was big news, and Davoll's arrest was noted in newspapers in Boston, New York, and elsewhere. Readers had been fascinated by the slave-trading case of Nathaniel Gordon, a merchant captain from Maine whose ship was seized by the USS *Mohican* off the coast of Africa with 897 slaves aboard. The capture occurred on August 8, 1860—at the same time that the *Brutus* was being fitted out at New Bedford. Gordon was indicted in New York, a city that had been very forgiving of slave traders, but the new Republican administration of Abraham Lincoln had brought in a team of district attorneys who were determined to break the complicity of indifferent judges, clever lawyers, and bought jurors who had seen to it that few slavers were convicted.[2]

Gordon—to the surprise of everyone, not least himself—was found guilty of the 1820 act that had defined slave trading

FIGURE 11. *The Hanging of Captain Gordon, Harper's Magazine,* March 8, 1862. Just as Captain Davoll was fitting out the false whaler *Brutus* in New Bedford in August 1860, Captain Nathaniel Gordon was captured by the U.S. Navy with 897 slaves aboard. His guilty verdict and execution had a chilling effect on the Atlantic slave trade. Courtesy of the New Bedford Whaling Museum.

as piracy, a capital crime. Even the usually softhearted president refused to issue a pardon. "I think I would personally prefer to let this man live in confinement and let him meditate on his deeds," Lincoln explained, "yet in the name of justice and the majesty of law, there ought to be one case, at least one specific instance, of a professional slave-trader, a Northern white man, given the exact penalty of death because of the incalculable number of deaths he and his kind inflicted upon black men amid the horror of the sea-voyage from Africa." On February 21, 1862, Gordon was hanged—the only person to be executed for slave trading in U.S. history.[3]

At the moment of Gordon's execution Davoll had been hiding out in Bermuda, where he likely read the startling news. Now that this new display of backbone by the federal district courts had chilled slave traders in the United States, any hope of the *Brutus* affair blowing over had become wishful thinking.

Up to this point, slaving had been relatively risk free, but with the *Brutus* story in the newspapers, Bigelow indicted, and now a slaving captain hanged, Davoll's engagement in the slave trade seems to have been, at the very least, ill-timed.

Davoll had been advised to stay in Bermuda until Bigelow's trial was over, but it was still in progress when the captain returned in June. Bigelow's prosecution dragged on for a very long time—as indicated by the ordeal of two witnesses. As noted earlier, Milo Robbins, the young crew member from Belchertown who had first brought the *Brutus* story to light, was detained in jail for 319 days. It was worse for Joseph Columbo, who endured 451 days as a witness. No wonder sailors on slaving voyages didn't talk about their experiences.[4]

The court proceedings are murky because of incomplete records, but the outline of events is clear. On July 1, 1862, Davoll was charged with having taken the *Brutus* to sea with the intention of slaving and was released after posting bond. On July 26 he was also charged with another crime. This was really a technicality and minor compared to the slave-trading accusation: he had not provided a certified crew list to the boarding officer at the first port of entry in the United States. The specific name that was missing was Milo Robbins. A captain was required to produce a list of all crew members going out and on entry a similar list, accounting for any men who were certified dead, absconded, or left at a foreign port. Davoll, "although often requested . . . wholly refused and neglected" to produce the list, for which he was fined $400—and which he repeatedly refused to pay. Apparently, paying would not have exonerated him from the more serious charge; otherwise, $400 would have been a small price to pay for his freedom.

In response to his obstinacy, the court commanded a federal marshal to attach his goods or estate for $1,000. (The same technicality and fine applied to Bigelow as well.) At home in New Bedford, Davoll received a summons to appear in Boston District Court on September 9.

Bigelow's trial proceeded, and despite his contention that he knew nothing of the illegal purpose of the ship he had purchased, he was fined $2,000 for "well knowing and intending that the said ship should be employed in the trade and business [of slaving]." Bigelow refused to pay any part of the fine and "although solemnly called to come into Court does not appear, but makes default."[5] This is the last we hear of Bigelow in the federal court records. Sometime after September 1862, he disappeared.

That left Davoll as the only principal participant in the *Brutus* affair still in the grasp of the federal court system. He was under indictment for taking the ship to sea with the intent of procuring slaves in Africa for transport and sale in Cuba and had refused to pay a $400 fine for failing to produce an accurate crew list of the *Brutus* voyage. There matters languished over the winter, until it all came to an end on April 15, 1863, when Edward Davoll died of typhoid fever in New Bedford at the age of forty.

During his career in whaling, especially after his marriage, Davoll had complained bitterly about the whaling life—the danger, the long absences from his wife and daughter, the lack of progress toward his financial goals. The last three years had been even worse, a time of anxiety over being found out, spending time at sea more to hide than to make financial progress, and enduring a drawn-out trial with poor prospects of exoneration. He was finally spending time with his family, but under a dark cloud—and in the end the intense pain and delirium of typhoid fever. There was no typhoid-fever epidemic in New Bedford at that time, although isolated cases were recorded. Davoll was one of the unlucky ones, and it's possible that his anxiety had left him vulnerable to the disease.[6]

We know nothing of his dying days or the anguish of Libby and eight-year-old Carrie. It's tempting to wonder if he made any connection to the suffering of the Africans in the disease-ridden hold of the *Brutus*. (Typhoid fever was one of the virulent diseases common on the Middle Passage.) Did he think of them and his role in their suffering? Probably not, although impending death can foster moments of terrible self-awareness. Certainly, he felt regret—for being caught, and perhaps something deeper, for having made terrible errors of judgment in trying to solve his financial challenges by engaging in the illegal slave trade.

The case against Captain Davoll was discontinued with no official determination, so what can be concluded about his guilt or innocence? The preponderance of evidence points to a guilty verdict. He had agreed to take command of a vessel owned by Pierre Pearce, a known slaver, and Albert Bigelow, a suspected sham owner of a slave ship. When suspicion was raised and broadcast in New Bedford newspapers, he did not back out; instead, he waited for the revenue cutter patrolling outside New Bedford harbor to leave and then rushed the *Brutus* through port customs and out to sea. And finally, obviously according to plan, he had departed the ship in the Azores, with his trunks, so there is no possibility of his first mate having wrested control of the ship and taken it on a slaving voyage that the captain knew nothing about. Davoll had done what he intended to do: fit out the *Brutus* to look like an authentic whaler and lend his name and reputation to provide legitimacy to an illegal venture. Once safely out of New Bedford, he could leave the dirty business of buying and selling slaves to others. The fact that he had stopped short of transporting slaves would not be sufficient to clear him; the law stipulated that any action that aided an intended slaving voyage was enough to warrant prosecution.

Davoll's previous involvement with slave trading on the *Atlantic* did not come out at his trial, but we know now that he played a role in that affair and very well might have taken the *Atlantic* to Africa if the Azores-based consul had not cleverly tricked him into returning to the United States. Even with the most generous interpretation of his activities, Davoll had at the very least abetted the slaving process, either ferrying ships or fitting them out in preparation for others to carry out the dreadful work of actually buying and selling slaves. The fact that Davoll had knowingly participated in the slave trade at least twice makes it difficult to escape the conclusion that he was guilty. But long before all of these pieces of his slave trading could be fit together, Davoll was dead and his prosecution cut short with no official verdict.

While it might seem unsatisfying to have no definitive trial judgment for Davoll, there is something fitting about the outcome: all of the principal actors in the *Brutus* affair managed to evade justice in the U.S. court system. Owner Pierre Pearce jumped bail and left the country. Sham owner Albert Bigelow also ran off and never returned to Massachusetts. William Jackson, the first mate, remained in Cuba after delivering his cargo of slaves. And Davoll died before judgment could be rendered. It's true that dying of typhoid fever is a poor way to escape justice, yet the fact that none of these men was successfully prosecuted is very typical of the vast majority of the hundreds of slaving voyages that took place after the first federal slave-trade ban went into effect in 1794. A few men were fined, a few went to prison (several received presidential pardons), and only one—Captain Gordon—was punished to the full extent of the law. In this respect, the voyage of the *Brutus* was all too typical.

CHAPTER 10

THE SHAM WHALERS OF
NEW BEDFORD

If the *Brutus* had been the only whaler-slaver to be fitted out in New Bedford, it could be considered an anomaly—and no threat to New Bedford's reputation as a bastion of antislavery sentiment. But Captain Davoll's experience was not unique in New Bedford. There were several other slave-trading voyages from the Whaling City between 1858 and 1861. These ventures, some successful in delivering slaves, some not, fill out the picture of how the slave trade operated and further explain the unusual connection between the slave trade and the whaling industry.

The voyages of the *Atlantic* show Davoll's earliest involvement in slaving and demonstrate how even the simple matter of ferrying a ship between ports was a vital part of the international slave trade. As related in chapter 6, the *Atlantic* had sailed from New Bedford in the summer of 1859 under the command of Francis J. Silva. At the Azores, Silva fell ill and Captain Davoll took command. Apparently, he was prepared to sail to Africa to purchase slaves but was diverted by the clever American consul into transporting displaced sailors to America. At some point Davoll left the ship and returned to New Bedford. The *Atlantic,* under a different captain, embarked on a successful slaving voyage.

About the same time that the *Atlantic* was leaving New Bedford, the 440-ton whaler *Comoro* arrived there from Boston. The owners of the ship were two Portuguese American master mariners, Francis J. Silva and José Maciel, who had also been involved in the *Atlantic* and had connections with the Portuguese slaving agents Abranches, Almeida & Co., operating out of New York. In July 1859 the *Comoro* cleared New Bedford under Captain Maciel and sometime in early 1860 delivered a cargo of slaves to Cuba. Despite suspicions, there were no arrests, and the *Comoro* later returned to New Bedford, where it was sold and the name changed to *Lady Young*. So even before the *Brutus* voyage, New Bedford had become an advantageous location for slavers like Silva and Maciel and their associated international agents and financiers to do business.[1]

An even earlier New Bedford slaving voyage shows that it wasn't just the Portuguese agents who targeted the city. In January 1859 Captain John B. Moody bought the 789-ton ship *Memphis* in New York and brought it to New Bedford to be fitted out for whaling. The co-owner was Andrew W. Fletcher of Sydney, Australia. Moody was a veteran of numerous voyages out of Sydney, so his connection to New Bedford was minimal. The *Whalemen's Shipping List* noted that the *Memphis* was the second-largest vessel ever fitted for whaling. A typical whaling vessel in 1859 was about 350 to 400 tons. An 800-ton behemoth brought in by outsiders ostensibly for whaling, at a time when the industry was in decline, should have raised suspicion.[2]

Yet the *Memphis* was fitted out at the New Bedford wharves, apparently without controversy, and cleared customs on February 26. While outfitted as a whaler, it had all the essential features of a slave ship. Formerly a packet, it had two passenger decks—perfect for carrying a very large number of slaves. And with boilers and wooden casks (ostensibly for rendering and storing whale oil), it would be able to provide food and water for the human cargo. On July 29, 1859, at Bahia Fonda, in present-day Angola, the ship came under surveillance by the British naval cruiser *Triton*. At three thirty in the morning the *Memphis* had anchored in shallow water a half mile from shore with a dozen local boats nearby. The suspected slaver was boarded by Lieutenant Burton of the *Triton*. He noted that the ship was only partially outfitted and had not engaged in whaling during its three months on the African coast. The captain of the *Memphis* produced what were undoubtedly false papers, but there was nothing the British officers could do to legally seize the vessel. An exasperated Lieutenant Burton knew all too well what would happen next: "I daily expect to hear that she has taken away about 1200 slaves from Bahia Fonda."[3] He was wrong only in the number: the *Memphis* took on 1,970 slaves and delivered 1,700 of them to Cárdenas, Cuba. The loss of 270 Africans en route to Cuba amounted to about 15 percent, which was, terrible to say, about average.[4]

The lieutenant expressed his frustration that American ships could not be stopped by the Royal Navy on mere suspicion; once they raised the U.S. flag and showed American papers (even if false), there was nothing the British could do. And he added another note of regret that British efforts at suppression of the slave trade sometimes led to an increase in deaths: "The many cases occurring similar to the above will assure you of the impunity with which slavers leave the United States, and the services of Her Majesty's cruizers causes the death of many hundreds of harmless wretches; for, while a cruizer remains in the neighbourhood of the barracoons where they are confined, the slaves are marched hurriedly to some other distant spot, and the mortality on these marches frequently amounts to some 10 or 20 per cent."[5]

These New Bedford–related slaving voyages—the *Comoro*, *Atlantic*, and *Memphis*, along with the *Brutus*—successfully landed slaves at Cuba. We don't know how many slaves were transported for all of these voyages, but using what data is available plus averages, a good estimate is about 3,500 Africans purchased in West Central Africa and 3,000 sold in Cuba. This appalling treatment of innocent men, women, and children was conceived by an international network of professional slave-trading agents and financiers and carried out by their accomplices. New

Bedford had not been a node of that network, but now agents were targeting the city, and there were men willing to abet the reprehensible trade. Two more ventures, although unsuccessful, will tell us a great deal more about how slave trading operated in New Bedford just prior to the Civil War.

The *Margaret Scott* voyage was organized by a man with the colorful name of Appleton Oaksmith. A New York businessman with shipping interests that included gun running to Latin America, Oaksmith was also an adventurer who supported William Walker's private military expedition in Central America in 1856. When Walker set himself up as president of Nicaragua, Oaksmith was his emissary to the United States. After that adventure ended in failure (Walker was executed in Honduras), Oaksmith's shipping business became entangled with the slave trade.[6] He was associated with John Albert Machado and his mistress, Mary Jane Watson, who were based in New York and part of a loose network referred to as the "Portuguese Company" with financial interest in the slaving voyages of both the *Atlantic* and the *Brutus,* among many others.[7]

In July 1860, Oaksmith traveled to New Bedford and, under an assumed name, began talking with men around the docks, trying to get a sense of who might be willing to engage in slaving. His inquiries led him to Ambrose Landre, a discredited former captain who now could find work only as a mate. Assessing him to be in need of money and indifferent to the slave trade, Oaksmith offered Landre $5,000 to help him find a suitable ship and take command. As a vulnerable small-time player in New Bedford whaling, Landre accepted the offer.

They went scouting for an appropriate vessel and found that the 330-ton whaling bark *Margaret Scott* was available. It was owned by Rodney French, a former mayor of New Bedford and an ardent abolitionist. Landre and French were acquainted, both owning shares in the whaler *Seine.* French would have been aware that Landre was not in robust financial shape, and it's curious that he didn't look more deeply into the matter be-fore selling. While it appears that French was out of town at the time and his son-in-law managed the transaction, French would certainly have been aware of the deal. It's possible that the negotiation was handled so skillfully that no suspicions were raised, or maybe it was a case of not wanting to know anything that might get in the way of the sale of an unwanted vessel.[8]

In any event, the ship was purchased for the bargain price of $2,400 with Landre as the intended owner. Landre balked—he already owned shares in a whaler that was losing money and feared that his creditors would come after his new acquisi-tion—so they brought in Samuel P. Skinner to be the registered owner. Skinner had been a whaling master but had run afoul of the New Bedford agents and owners. In 1850, on a whaling voyage in the Pacific, he had taken his vessel to San Francisco and abandoned it to join the Gold Rush. (William Jackson, first mate under Davoll on the *Brutus,* had done the same thing.) Having failed to make his fortune in California, Skinner re-turned to New Bedford but was unable to regain his former status. An outcast in his chosen profession and short of money, he was ripe for exploitation by slaving agents. The $5,000 pay-out would be a lifesaver.[9]

Furthermore, it would not be difficult to find a crew, given the extraordinary financial rewards, typically $1,500 for mates and $500 for ordinary seamen. While there were some sailors who specifically looked for slaving voyages, many were un-aware when they put out to sea. Ambrose Landre was told by Oaksmith not to inform the crew before the voyage: "It would not do for any one, officers or men, to know the ship was going to the Coast of Africa. Mr. Oaksmith said everything would be made right when we came there to the Coast. They would all come into it, they always did."[10]

Oaksmith provided Skinner with money that he deposited in his own name in a New Bedford bank. The outfitting of the ship was minimal—no repairs or new rigging, no new whaling gear. A careful inspection would have indicated the ship's unfitness for an extended cruise, but there was nothing to specifically identify it as a slaver and the *Margaret Scott* was able to clear customs. But federal authorities, aware of Oaksmith's past, had been watching the process, and when the ship left the harbor on September 3 it was seized by a U.S. Revenue cutter and returned to New Bedford. Skinner and Landre were arrested on the federal offense of intending to engage in the slave trade.

The law had always specified that any intended involvement in slave trading was enough for prosecution, but for the most part arrests were made only when slaves had been purchased and were still on board. The *Margaret Scott* case indicates how the climate had changed after the Lincoln administration had undertaken, as the *New York Times* put it, "to displace officials derelict of their duty, and appoint others competent and disposed to energetically enforce laws for which they were appointed."[11] Federal prosecutors were also fortunate that Ambrose Landre agreed to testify against his partners.

There was plenty of evidence of intent: a thousand barrels of fresh water had been loaded, the ship was provisioned with beef that "no ship owner in New Bedford would take as a gift," the whaling gear was inadequate, and there was no spare rigging. Most damning of all, Skinner could not explain how he suddenly came into possession of so much money. There was another interesting bit of evidence: Oaksmith had purchased the New Bedford whaling bark *Manuel Ortez* and dispatched it under Skinner's command to New York to be loaded with rum and tobacco; from there it sailed to the west coast of Africa to rendezvous with the *Margaret Scott* and act as its supply ship. Although seized as a suspected auxiliary in the slave trade, the *Manuel Ortez* was released because the projected rendezvous never occurred, but its connection to the planned slaving voyage was clear.[12]

Landre and Skinner were tried and convicted, and both went to prison. Skinner was prosecuted by the indefatigable Richard Henry Dana Jr., the district attorney for the Massachusetts District Court. Appointed by the Lincoln administration and expected to vigorously prosecute slave traders, Dana proved his mettle. Skinner's sentence of five years at hard labor and $1,000 fine was the first severe penalty for *intent* to engage in slaving.[13] Little is known about Landre's fate. He probably got a reduced sentence because of his willingness to testify against Skinner and Oaksmith.

Oaksmith was also found guilty on seven counts. His slaving activities in New York—for which he had managed to evade prosecution—had been followed by U.S. Marshal Robert Murray, who traveled to Boston for the *Margaret Scott* proceedings. When Oaksmith was found guilty, Murray wrote, "I consider his conviction of greater triumph in the cause of the suppression of the Slave Trade than the execution of Gordon the slaver captain." However, to the dismay of everyone who had looked forward to his richly deserved punishment, Oaksmith managed to escape from the Suffolk County Jail and spent the rest of his life a free man.[14]

On the surface, it was not a particularly just outcome, with only Skinner receiving the maximum punishment. Yet Skinner's conviction and substantial sentence marked an important development in the suppression of the slave trade. Captain Gordon had been punished more severely, but he had been captured on his fourth slaving voyage with 897 slaves on board. Skinner's conviction demonstrated that buying or fitting out a vessel with the intention to slave (even if unsuccessful) was going to be prosecuted vigorously and would result in a long prison term. Samuel Skinner's sentence and Nathaniel Gordon's execution were important deterrents to the slave trade. As the British consul at Boston commented on the new activism of the attorneys general and the particular effect of this trial, "It would seem that the United States Government are determined to energetically repress this horrible traffic. There is little doubt but that this sentence on Captain Skinner will deter many who have hitherto enjoyed impunity from repeating their ventures."[15]

One more whaler was fitted out for slaving in New Bedford in 1860. The *Tahmaroo,* a vessel from the adjoining port town of Fairhaven, was purchased in June by Zeno Kelley, a New Bedford jewelry-shop owner. Kelley was also active in the whaling industry as partial owner of twelve vessels during the 1850s.[16] Following the established slaving procedure of obscuring ownership, the *Tahmaroo* was registered in the name of Captain Jabez Hathaway. A master of at least two New Bedford whaling voyages, Hathaway had been captain of the *Sally Anne* when it was wrecked on a reef in the Friendly Islands (present-day Tonga) in the South Pacific in April 1854. Although the captain claimed the accident was not his fault (the island was "not laid down correctly in the chart"), it is likely that he lost the confidence of the New Bedford whaling agents and owners. Like Captains Skinner and Landre of the *Margaret Scott,* Hathaway was in a position to be lured by the easy money of the slave trade. The first mate was Luther Whittemore (or Whitmore), a veteran of at least three whaling voyages from New Bedford.[17]

On July 3, 1860, the 371-ton *Tahmaroo,* properly fitted out for whaling, cleared New Bedford customs. Once out to sea, a number of new crew members came aboard (a trick to avoid official shipping papers), and a "passenger" named John C. Cook took command of the ship. It appears that Hathaway's main role was, like Captain Davoll's, to get the vessel through customs. The *Tahmaroo* stopped at the Azores and then made for the Cape Verde Islands, where it was met by the schooner *Thriver,* acting as a supply ship (in the same manner that the *Manuel Ortez* was intended to supply the *Margaret Scott*). The *Thriver* carried a large quantity of rice and $3,000 in gold, clear indications of a slaving voyage. Reaching the coast of Africa,

Cook went ashore and bargained for slaves. Offered only four hundred captives when he needed eleven hundred to meet his profit goal, Cook left the coast and returned to the Azores. A stop at Cuba to set up a potential sale was followed by another unsuccessful negotiation in Africa, after which the *Tahmaroo* returned to the Azores where Hathaway—still aboard and the nominal owner—sold the ship, thus eliminating the primary evidence of attempted slaving.

But there were suspicions, and when Hathaway and Whittemore returned to Massachusetts they were arrested, along with Zeno Kelley. At an examination by the commissioner in New Bedford, the charges were dismissed due to lack of evidence. Hathaway, frightened by the close call, fled the country. Later, when John Cook returned, he also became fearful and escaped to Canada. Whittemore, however, turned state's evidence, and a grand jury indicted Kelley, Hathaway, and Cook. By the time of the trial, Whittemore had jumped bail, other witnesses were "spirited away," and the case against the *Tahmaroo* slavers collapsed.

The district attorney at Boston, Richard Henry Dana Jr., was undeterred. Early in 1862, two crew members of the *Tahmaroo*, one Portuguese and one Hawaiian, came forward as witnesses. The Hawaiian, Keaupuni (known aboard ship as Joe Mowee), was particularly effective. Having spent time on a cargo ship in the Pacific in his younger days (related in his popular book *Two Years before the Mast*), Dana had developed great respect for the Hawaiian sailors he met and worked with and was very successful in bringing out Keaupuni's damaging testimony. Kelley was convicted in April 1863 for outfitting a slaver, but the conviction was appealed and overturned on a technicality.[18]

Dana, again with Keaupuni's credible testimony, then went after the captain who had taken over command of the *Tahmaroo*, John Cook, who had been tracked down in New York. Facing six counts, Cook pleaded guilty to the lesser charge of "being employed upon a vessel engaged in the slave trade," and the other charges were dropped. On June 4 Cook was sentenced to two years in the New Bedford jail and a $5 fine. Three months later, Dana had Zeno Kelley rearrested, and this time he was found guilty of fitting out a vessel with the intent to engage in the slave trade. He was sentenced to four years in jail and fined $1,000.[19]

There was an outpouring of sentiment in favor of a presidential pardon for Kelley, supported by leading citizens of New Bedford and even his jailers. Kelley claimed he was in poor health, that his family was being punished, and that he was innocent. One supporter wrote to President Lincoln that Kelley was innocent "as sure as there is a God in Heaven." Dana knew better. Not only was Kelley guilty, but behind the scenes he had been blackmailing two New Bedford citizens who had backed him in purchasing the *Tahmaroo*. Urged by the Massachusetts congressional delegation, Lincoln agreed to a pardon, but it was held up by the State Department. Following Lincoln's assassination in April 1865, Kelley's supporters appealed to the new president, Andrew Johnson, but Dana stood strongly in opposition, calling the Kelley case "one of complete villainy." (He had discovered that three of the men who clamored for Kelley's pardon had been investors in the *Tahmaroo;* they were found guilty and fined. Another man, Antoine Thomas, admitted to aiding in the fitting out of the slaver and bribing witnesses to keep them from testifying in Kelley's trial.)[20] In Attorney Dana's summary, "[Kelley] was not only guilty of fitting out a slaver from New Bedford, but of a long series of acts suborning and spiriting away witnesses, buying off parties and witnesses, and concealing and protecting the wealthier parties behind him, and at the same time exacting black mail from them." Yet after Kelley had served three years of his sentence, Dana supported his pardon because Kelley had been an important informant against others involved in the purchase and outfitting of the slaver.[21]

The *Tahmaroo* case was an important trial in the history of the slave trade. As with the *Margaret Scott,* no slaves had been purchased, transported, or sold, but now the fitting out of a ship with the intention of trading in slaves—illegal for decades— was finally enough to merit and receive harsh punishment. It was the last slave ship fitted out in New Bedford.

That is how the slave trade operated in the Whaling City. A well-financed international ring of traders in Portugal, Spain, Brazil, Cuba, and New York funneled money to agents and middlemen, who looked for shipowners who were anxious to unload their money-losing vessels and found unscrupulous men who would register as owner for a cut of the profits. These local owners would then procure down-on-their-luck captains and mates to run the ship—or simply to add the legitimacy necessary to pass through customs (Davoll and Skinner both turned over command of their vessels once cleared of New Bedford). Outfitters were willing to prepare the ship for whaling, even under suspicious circumstances—they could always claim it appeared to be a legitimate whaler. The various workmen and provisioners, always looking for work in an uncertain economy, could ignore the rumors and look the other way; they were just trying to make a living.

These voyages of the *Atlantic, Brutus, Memphis, Comoro, Margaret Scott,* and *Tahmaroo* reveal how the slave trade operated from a whaling port. But this only partially answers *why* men would engage in such a vile enterprise. Furthermore, how could it take place in a bastion of antislavery sentiment like New Bedford?

CHAPTER 11

SLAVE TRADERS
AND ABOLITIONISTS

Six false whalers were fitted out in New Bedford in 1859 and 1860. We have seen how the operation worked, with outside funding, devious agents, sham owners, and mariners whose desire for money overcame their moral scruples and who would fit out, provision, and sail on a suspected slaver. Even the elite of the whaling industry, the owners and agents, were slow to recognize the threat to their moral standing and that of their city with its reputation as a model of race relations in the North and a stronghold of antislavery sentiment. The reputation was real, but it hid a darker side.

It isn't news that Northerners were complicit in slavery. New York became the center for the slave trade in the United States in the mid-nineteenth century, with sixty slaving voyages from its ports between 1850 and 1866, mostly to Cuba. The city was also the financial center of the cotton trade, and proslavery sentiment was commonplace—to the point that Mayor Fernando Wood proposed on the eve of the Civil War that New York secede from the Union. The very existence of the city, Wood claimed, depended on "the continuance of slave labor and the prosperity of the slave master!"[1]

But New York wasn't alone. New Englanders had played an important part in the slave trade since the seventeenth century. Puritans—those exemplars of virtue—began shipping African slaves to Barbados as early as 1645. Mariners from Rhode Island, particularly the D'Wolf family of Bristol, made fortunes in the notorious "triangle trade," exchanging locally distilled rum for African slaves whom they transported to the West Indies to be traded for molasses to distill more rum, which funded the next voyage around the triangle.[2] Even those New Englanders not directly involved in slavery profited by trading with the West Indian plantations whose owners were so focused on sugar that they needed to import food for their slaves. As historian Bernard Bailyn summarized, "Slavery was the ultimate source of the commercial economy of eighteenth-century New England. Only a few of New England's merchants actually engaged in the slave trade, but all of them profited by it, lived off it."[3]

Cotton also played a role. By the early nineteenth century, New England textile manufacturers established strong ties to cotton producers in the South. Faced with growing antislavery sentiment, the textile magnates came under fire. There was only one successful cotton mill in New Bedford before the Civil War, so textile manufacturing had yet to dominate the city's economy as it would later in the century. But for the city's moneyed elite who had begun to invest their whaling fortunes in textiles, the 1850s was no time to antagonize the South. If the cotton industrialists were against slavery, they were not among the radicals.

Yet New Bedford could justly be proud of its race relations and opposition to slavery. Antislavery societies were formed in the early 1830s. The great abolitionist Frederick Douglass had found a home there after escaping from bondage in 1838. The Underground Railroad was vigorous and successful. An early historian of the city, Daniel Ricketson, wrote in 1858, "The number of the colored population of New Bedford has always been large, and has increased proportionally with the growth of the place. At present there are probably between two and three thousand, many of them among our most respectable and worthy citizens, and in their general character, as a whole, remarkable for their morality, industry, and thrift. . . . Owing to the early influence of the anti-slavery principles of the Society of Friends, there is but little prejudice against color."[4]

This appraisal is true—up to a point. If New Bedford provided the first home for Frederick Douglass as a free man, it is also true that he was denied work as a ship caulker, a job for which he was well qualified, because white caulkers refused to work alongside him. Offsetting the positive stories of black success and integrated schools were incidents of job discrimination, arson that targeted black homes and businesses, and social isolation. New Bedford's black citizens lived in the two poorest wards, while the city's elite had moved away from the waterfront to the high ground of County Street. The wealth and elegance were real, but New Bedford was also home to seventy-eight liquor stores and fifty-six "houses of ill repute" in the 1850s. The veneer of respectability and racial openness concealed a more typical antebellum Northern city, with its social and economic tensions. Still, it was preferable to most places in the North. As Frederick Douglass put it, "Here in New Bedford, it was my good fortune to see a pretty near approach to freedom on the part of the colored people."[5]

In his history of New Bedford, Ricketson credited the Society of Friends (Quakers) for the city's "general willingness and desire that the colored population may enjoy equal rights and privileges with themselves." Yet Quaker authority had been waning for decades: between 1845 and 1855, the number of Quakers in town had dropped from 600 to 267, as internal schisms lessened membership and influence. One New Bedford former fugitive slave said about the Friends, "They will give us good advice. They will aid in giving us a partial education—but never in a Quaker school, beside their own children. Whatever they do for us savors of pity, and is done at arm's length." The Quaker relationship to abolitionism is complex, but to some degree they were taking a principled stand: Friends had always been guided by nonviolence, and as abolitionism became more confrontational, they retreated. This is not to say that Quakers did not contribute to the antislavery movement—Quakers were largely responsible for driving the infamous D'Wolf family out of the Bristol, Rhode Island, slave trade, and the Rotches, Rodmans, and Ricketson himself, among other leading New Bedford Friends, were active abolitionists. Still, the early Quaker influence had diminished.[6]

Quakers were only one of several religious societies in the city. Antislavery leaders were critical of the reluctance of New Bedford's churches to take a leadership role in the abolition movement, which highlights a contradiction: churches were often the driving force behind the antislavery cause, while at the same time retarding progress. This sentiment was echoed by Deborah Weston, one of the founders of the Boston Female Anti-slavery Society, who noted that the "wharves and churches" of New Bedford were not aligned with the movement.[7] Other Protestant churches, aside from black congregations, were generally either uncommitted to abolition or conservative in their approach. Weston complained that, despite her entreaties, the ministers of the Congregational and Episcopal churches would not read announcements of upcoming antislavery events. The Elm Street Methodist Church was integrated and the first church Frederick Douglass attended as a free man in New Bedford, but when he was told to sit in the colored section, he walked out "and have never been in that church since."[8]

Most Christians were "gradualists" who opposed the radicals' demand for immediate emancipation. Mainstream Protestant organizations like the American Bible Society and the American Sunday School Union denounced abolitionists as dangerous agitators. New Bedford's white churches were not in the vanguard of social change; abolition might bring a reversal of the social order—might promote interracial marriage—and that was altogether too radical. (An exception was John Overton Chules, pastor of New Bedford's First Baptist Church, who was an ardent abolitionist and a founder of the New Bedford Antislavery Society.)[9] Black churches became more militant in the 1850s and urged their parishioners to have no "connection or sympathy with slaveholders, their apologist churches, ministers, or members, whether they be white or black."[10] This might have further distanced the white congregations.

The antislavery movement in America became much more radical after the passage of the Fugitive Slave Act in 1850. This act stipulated that slaves who escaped to free states must be returned to their masters and that citizens and law enforcement officials who provided food or shelter to runaways or simply did not cooperate with federal marshals could be prosecuted. By forcing free-state citizens to act on behalf of slaveholders, the Fugitive Slave Act made the issue of slavery less abstract—something that one could treat with indifference—and more a reality that demanded action.

It was this radicalization of the antislavery movement that polarized opinion in town. Rodney French (a former mayor of New Bedford and owner of the whaler *Margaret Scott*) provides an example of the kind of abolitionists that more moderate citizens feared. After the Fugitive Slave Act was passed, French declared the law to be "the most disgraceful, atrocious, unjust, detestable, heathenish, barbarous, diabolical, tyrannical, man-degrading, woman-murdering, demon-pleasing, heaven-defying act ever perpetrated in any age of the world by persons claiming to have consciences and a belief in a just God." French was widely despised by his more genteel and socially conservative neighbors. Even staunch antislavery advocates distanced themselves from abolitionists. Few did more to suppress the slave trade than Richard Henry Dana Jr., yet Dana considered the renowned abolitionist William Lloyd Garrison a "fanatic," whose "heated, narrow minded, self-willed, excited, unchristian radical energies set to work upon a cause which is good, if rightly managed, but which [abolitionists] have made a hot bed."[11] As Orville Dewey, a New Bedford Unitarian minister, put it, "Almost every respectable and influential man who comes before the public, whether in speech or print, to declare his protest against slavery . . . takes pains to say that he is not an abolitionist. Men avoid the name as they would a pestilence."[12]

Underlying these tensions was a deep-seated racial prejudice that pervaded the country. Nearly all whites in the North believed in black social and political inferiority. Most public institutions were closed to black Americans: as William Lloyd Garrison put it, "Hardly any doors but those of our State Prisons were open to our colored brethren."[13] The widely held belief in black intellectual inferiority was supported by the science of the time. In classifying the races of mankind, whites were always placed at the top and blacks at the bottom. Many believed that black-skinned people had been created separately from other human beings and were by nature, and in the eyes of God, inferior. As a U.S. Navy lieutenant who had rescued a cargo of slaves described the Africans, "Physically they were men and women, but otherwise as far removed from the Anglo-Saxon as the oyster from the baboon, or the mole from the horse." The majority of Americans would have agreed.[14]

Even abolitionists could be guilty of racial prejudice. As one black antislavery leader chided his fellow advocates, "It is an easy thing to ask about the vileness of slavery in the South, but to call the dark man a brother . . . that is the test." Another pleaded with his colleagues to eliminate "prejudice from their own hearts." Historian Ricketson, a New Bedford native, captured the social inequality perfectly: "A colored person, even of the deepest dye, may stand by our chair while at meals and wait upon us—may cook our food—ay! put their dark hands into our bread—tend and nurse our children, and nothing is thought of it—but to sit near us in a concert room, a lecture room, or a church, this is by no means to be thought of."[15]

Racial prejudice may have been even more widespread on the waterfront. Black mariners had once been respected in the whaling industry, and while most remained stewards or ordinary seamen, there were many cases of advancement to mate and even to captain (recall that Edward Davoll's first voyage in 1840 had been under the command of a successful black captain, Pardon Cook). But by the 1850s, with an influx of white immigrants willing to go to sea, and fewer professional sailors climbing the ranks, black sailors were increasingly relegated to the menial jobs, and respect eroded. New Bedford was a typical port city where the harsh reality of race relations played out regardless of the high-minded rhetoric of the city leaders.[16]

The poorer wards and the waterfront were populated by dockworkers, sailors, ship carpenters, boardinghouse keepers, provisioners, and others who worked in the seafaring trades. Many were transients. Many were immigrants, especially the Irish. Many were unemployed. The competition for jobs was fierce, especially during the hard economic times of the late 1850s. These men were less likely to be interested in receiving lessons in antislavery from their betters or sympathizing with the African Americans with whom they competed for work. (One persistent fear about abolitionism was that immediate emancipation would bring a flood of low-wage black laborers to Northern cities, where they would drive white laborers into unemployment.) The people of the waterfront didn't write much or express their opinions in newspapers, didn't belong to the churches that promoted abolition or to antislavery societies. While many had steady employment and some made it to the ranks of the solid middle class of New Bedford, they weren't among the leading citizens of the city and in fact resented the wealthy families who ran the businesses and lived high on the hill. It would be unfair to categorize such a large and varied group of people on their attitude toward slavery, but it is likely that few were radical abolitionists. Among the waterfront's local whites, blacks, Irish, and other immigrants, there was little time or inclination for elite concerns like antislavery when there was such a struggle for jobs and plenty of opportunity for resentment. This atmosphere of poverty, anger, racial tension, and indifference could be easily exploited by a shrewd slaving agent.

Of course, not all waterfront inhabitants would engage in the slave trade; most were good men and women trying to make an honest living, and there was some attempt to blame outsiders— "those desperate adventurers and reckless sailors who infest our large seaports." This is partially true: rootless sailors with no ties to a community and little education were more likely to engage in slaving. But it ignores the "better sort" of the whaling industry: captains, outfitters, and investors (Davoll, Bigelow, Kelley) who were not transient and had standing in the community. The blame went beyond outsiders and the lowly.[17]

And it went beyond the conventional racism of the time as well. Certainly, Captain Davoll was what we would today call racist. He held the Portuguese of the Azores in low regard. He called his cook "the Darkie" instead of using his name, as he did with white sailors. And it's hard to dismiss his chilling description of Australian Aborigines as "horrid dirty objects."[18] Yet his prejudice was probably no worse than average for his time. Despite widespread racism, most people from Westport or New Bedford did not get involved in the slave trade—that is, their prejudice did not impel them to do harm to people of color. Slavers didn't necessarily hate Africans but felt such contempt for them that exploitation was easy to justify. In fact, it wasn't only Africans; during this same period, Chinese "coolies" were being transported to Cuba by the thousands to work as "free laborers" on the sugar plantations. The conditions were virtually indistinguishable from slavery, yet the public was largely apathetic.[19]

But it appears that when an opportunity to make a great deal of money arose, and it involved Africans, a man could inflict harm he would never direct toward a person he considered one of his own kind. The victim was distant and disconnected, not seen as a fellow human being worthy of empathy—or that simply shouldn't be abused. The slaving agents were paying good money to men who would fit out or sail on vessels that would transport "cargo" that happened to consist of human beings but of a marginalized race. People the world over craved sugar, Cuba produced one-third of the supply worldwide, expanding plantations were desperate for cheap labor, and there were plenty of individuals to play their part in the slaving network, lured by easy money and morally shielded by their indifference to the suffering of people who weren't like them. For some, the economic opportunity could not be resisted.[20]

If the diverse and messy waterfront environment of New Bedford was not much different from other ports in the North, what was it about this city that made it so appealing to the agents of the slave trade? The main factor, already noted earlier, is the suitability of a large whaling vessel for slaving. The ample hold could accommodate hundreds of tightly packed slaves. Barrels intended for whale oil could be used for fresh water. The tryworks boilers, for rendering whale blubber, were easily adapted to cooking rice. Even professionals couldn't always distinguish a whaler from a slaver, so getting through port customs was not particularly difficult. Once at sea, the crew would occasionally chase whales, mostly for show to confound the navy. And because the west coast of Africa was a legitimate whaling ground, it was not unusual for a whaler to be in the vicinity of the known slaving areas. It was a nearly perfect disguise.

This doesn't mean whaling vessels were the first choice of the slaving agents. Whalers were slow when speed was of the essence both to evade the Royal or U.S. Navy and to get from Africa to Cuba as quickly as possible to minimize deaths in passage. Slave traders preferred fast clipper ships, but those were more easily identified as slavers, and as scrutiny increased in the late 1850s, the disguise factor of whaling vessels became more important. New York had been the base for the majority of slaving voyages throughout the 1850s, and agents were looking for less suspicious ports. As the center of whaling, and previously unconnected with the slave trade, New Bedford became a prime target.

New Bedford was also economically appealing to slavers because of the decline in the whaling business. It had been a given that the city's success would go on forever; as one historian of the time summarized, "From the year 1820 until the year 1857 her prosperity and her accumulation of wealth were continuous almost without exception."[21] Despite the busy wharves and ten thousand sailors employed in the industry, the decline was evident to anyone who read the local newspapers. Whales had become more scarce, voyages longer, and it was becoming harder for all but the wealthiest owners and agents to make a profit. As the *Whalemen's Shipping List* reported in 1858, "Of the sixty-eight whalers expected to arrive at New Bedford and Fairhaven the present year, forty-four will actually make losing voyages—some from the small amount of oil taken, and others from the low price of oil and bone, now ruling, which otherwise would have made 'saving voyages.' This is certainly a gloomy prospect, but nevertheless true."[22]

Compounding the decline in whaling was the financial panic of 1857. The good economic times of the early 1850s, fueled by California gold, easy credit, and railroad expansion, led to overextension and wild speculation. Banks began calling in loans, and as credit tightened businesses without deep resources failed and unemployment rose precipitously. Whaling didn't end: there were profits to be made, but the men with capital resources managed much better than the small outfits. The glut of ships depressed prices, and slaving agents saw an opportunity to buy up cheap vessels, which lowered their cost of doing business. Even as the economy began to recover from the 1857 downturn, the *Whalemen's Shipping List* reported that the decline was not temporary: "Those who have the best opportunities for judging correctly think that this falling off will be permanent."[23]

And then, in 1859, the whaling industry was staggered by the discovery of oil by Edwin Drake in Titusville, Pennsylvania. By the end of that year, Drake's well produced eighty-four thousand gallons of crude oil, at about thirty-eight cents per gallon. A year later, more than two hundred wells in Titusville were producing twenty-one million gallons at about twenty-three cents per gallon. At double the price, how could whale oil compete? This should not have come as a surprise: kerosene had been a substitute illuminant for some time—it was even produced locally on New Bedford's Fish Island—but until now it had been more expensive. Another earlier sign was the decision in 1852 to convert the city's streetlights to gas, a blow to "the city that lit the world" with whale oil. By early 1860, New Bedford shipowners had resorted to offering prizes to encourage the development of special lamps that would burn whale oil better than kerosene in an attempt to promote their most valuable product over its new competitor. All but the most optimistic boosters of whaling knew that the trend was not in the industry's favor.[24]

GRAND BALL GIVEN BY THE WHALES IN HONOR OF THE DISCOVERY OF THE OIL WELLS IN PENNSYLVANIA.

FIGURE 12. *Grand Ball Given by the Whales in Honor of the Discovery of Oil in Pennsylvania.* When oil was discovered in Pennsylvania in 1859, the whaling industry suffered a severe blow. Kerosene made from petroleum was much cheaper than whale oil. This clever cartoon was published in *Vanity Fair* in 1861. Courtesy of the New Bedford Whaling Museum.

While whaling could still be profitable, some of the leading capitalists had begun to invest in the emerging textile industry. New Bedford's first large cotton mill, the Wamsutta, opened in 1849, added a huge second mill in 1855, and led the way to rapid industrialization in the city after the Civil War. The capitalists had a new and productive place for their money. Those who remained tied to the whaling industry, particularly the seafaring men and maritime suppliers, would suffer. Whaling captains, who had for decades become wealthy and often transitioned into roles as agents or owners in midlife, were facing the prospect of longer voyages, lower earnings, and fewer opportunities for shore-based income. Captain Edward Davoll had reached a critical point in his career at precisely the wrong time.[25]

Amid this gloom for New Bedford's seafaring interests, there loomed the dubious alternative of the slave trade. Compared to whaling (or any other maritime enterprise), it was hugely profitable. A slave could be purchased for $50 on the coast of Africa and sold for $500 to $1,000 in Cuba. Subtracting the cost of the ship, crew wages, a 10 to 15 percent loss of slaves in transit, bribes, and other expenses, the delivery of five hundred slaves could easily bring a 100 percent profit.[26] One merely had to get over the moral opprobrium and illegality, which some apparently did with little difficulty. The risk of prosecution was not a great concern, as most slavers got through the port authorities by means of bribes, and surveillance by the U.S. Navy's African Squadron was largely ineffective.[27] In the few cases of arrest, the trial typically ended in acquittal. Corruption of officials, the cleverness of expensive defense attorneys—some of whom specialized in defending accused slavers—and the indifference of judges and juries to the plight of African slaves usually won the day. The owners and outfitters of slavers disguised as whaling vessels bypassed most of these obstacles: they didn't need to bribe officials when their slave ship was indistinguishable from a legitimate whaler.

The money was easy and plentiful. The agents of the trade found men like Skinner, Landre, and the *Brutus* mate Jackson by hanging around the docks and asking a few questions. These mariners had all been discredited, and their lowered status had affected them financially. Davoll was not exactly in disgrace—he seems to have put the *Iris* shipwreck behind him, and he was still a captain—but he was disillusioned by the decline in whaling and his diminishing prospects of retiring from a life at sea. Men like Albert Bigelow (of the *Brutus*) and Zeno Kelley (of the *Tahmaroo*) were small-time businessmen, probably suffering from the contraction of whaling and the hard financial times, and had been willing to act as sham owners of slaving vessels. And remember that Kelley had three financial backers, men of good reputation in New Bedford. Money, made quickly and with little effort and (until recently) with minimal risk, was certainly a critical factor in drawing otherwise solid citizens into the slave trade. The slaving agents didn't care if these men were discredited in the eyes of New Bedford's elite; in fact, they were able to prey upon them for that very reason.

To many in the maritime trades, particularly in hard economic times, the slave trade could be seen as just another business. It existed, and someone was going to make money from it, so why not seize the opportunity? This attitude had been clearly expressed by the Providence shipping magnate and slave trader John Brown (brother of Quaker abolitionist Moses Brown), reacting to the federal ban on the slave trade in 1794: "Why should we see Great Britain getting all the slave trade to themselves? Why may not our country be enriched by that lucrative trade?"[28] Mariners made their living transporting various sorts of cargo from one place to another. The cargo could be fish, barrels of whale oil, flour—or Africans. In this respect slaves were treated like cattle, a live cargo to be herded onto a ship, kept alive in transit in order to maximize profit, and delivered to another port. Some loss was to be expected and factored into the profit calculation. An indication of this view is a remark made by Captain Gordon, the slaver who was executed in 1862, who claimed during his trial, "I have no trouble of conscience. I never harmed a human being in my life." An African slave was not a human being but a commodity—in the terminology of the day, "black gold."[29]

Many of the men who engaged in the slave trade were able to keep their hands clean of the actual buying and selling of human beings. Captain Davoll never encountered a slave. His role in the complex slaving network was to clear a ship from a port (New Bedford) or transport a ship to another port (Azores to New York) to be fitted for slaving. In the case of the *Brutus,* it is likely that he never intended to go to Africa—that is, relinquishing command to his first mate in the Azores had been prearranged. This was a common practice: a captain would get the vessel past the customs officials and then turn over command to an experienced slaver, often Spanish in the case of the Cuban trade. This served two purposes. The division of labor assigned each man to what he did best. Davoll had no experience buying slaves in Africa, so that role went to a Spanish captain who had done it before. Davoll knew how to outfit a legitimate whaler and get it out of New Bedford Harbor, so that was his assigned role. A secondary benefit was that Davoll could comfort himself that he had not engaged in buying slaves. His conscience was clear: his only involvement was the ordinary business of outfitting and ferrying ships.

Not everyone agreed that working on the edges of the slave trade was proper. An editorial in the *New York World* of August 29, 1860 (the day after the *Brutus* sailed from New Bedford), could have been a direct reference to Davoll's role. "Is it any moral difference in a Captain taking a vessel to the Western Islands [Azores] and transferring her to others—though clearing her for a whaling voyage—and going to the Coast [of Africa]? The difference is, one is direct, the other is indirect, the result is the same."[30] Legally and morally, the editorial captured Davoll's situation perfectly.

Despite the occasional editorial condemning any level of involvement in slaving, much public opinion was on the slavers' side. As the *New York Herald* asked late in 1861, wasn't slaving just "the mere violation of a commercial law"? Maritime men had often skirted regulations—underreporting cargo or evading duties, for example—and playing a marginal role in the illegal trade could appear to be a minor infraction to those trying to justify their involvement. As another New York newspaper commented, it appeared that slave-trade laws were treated with the same impunity as the city's liquor laws. To many, participation in slaving did not rise to the level of a serious moral or legal transgression.[31]

Defenders of the slave trade could also fall back on a terrible legal contradiction with regard to slavery: in America it was perfectly lawful to purchase a slave in one state and sell him in another. That is, there was no prohibition on the *internal* slave trade. In banning the transatlantic slave trade in 1808, legislators from the upper South, which had a surplus of slaves, agreed with Northern congressmen to end the importation of new slaves from Africa. Eliminating this competition maintained a high price for slaves already in America, as they were sold "down the river" to plantations in the Deep South. If a slave could be bought in Virginia and sold in New Orleans, some argued, what could be wrong with transporting slaves from Africa to Cuba?

Americans of the mid-nineteenth century lived in a morally confused political culture in which slavery was legal in half the country. The average Northerner was not an abolitionist, was mildly against slavery but highly prejudiced toward people of color, and generally indifferent to an issue that did not concern his or her everyday life. Those who became entangled in the slave trade—a small minority, to be sure—were products of their culture but also had a financial need and a moral shallowness that allowed them to be drawn in and perhaps to rationalize their own behavior. The predators who made up the professional ranks of the slave trade—the agents and financiers like Pierre Pearce, Appleton Oaksmith, and John Machado— made their living organizing the buying and selling of human beings and preyed on men like Davoll, Skinner, and other morally weak mariners who would aid them.

If we can imagine Edward Davoll as he might have projected himself in the future, he would be a man of comfortable means in his own home in Westport or New Bedford, one of the better sort in town, managing his substantial investments in whaling vessels. One indication is his acceptance, in January 1859, into the Star of the East Masonic Lodge, an organization composed of the established and up-and-coming businessmen of New Bedford. But in reality Davoll occupied an anomalous position somewhere between the solid whaling businessmen in town and the struggling seamen of the waterfront. In title he was closer to the elite, a professional master mariner, but his dream of wealth and status was slipping away. The moneymakers of 1860 were more likely to be owners, agents, and shrewd investors. Davoll was a working captain and a minor investor but had never made enough to become financially secure or even to own his own home. A revealing comparison is Edward C. Jones, Davoll's agent on the *Iris* voyage, whose real and personal property were valued at $223,000 in 1855.[32] The captain was not in the same league.

In many ways, Davoll identified more with the common sailors who made up his crews. This is evident in a letter he wrote to his wife during his first voyage as captain of the *Cornelia*. It is an earnest and impassioned defense of seamen who have been exploited by owners, outfitters, and recruiters who "fleece their pockets of what few Coppers they have ventured their lives for."[33] Davoll had come up through the ranks and empathized with the plight of ordinary seamen and had little regard for the wealthy businessmen of the whaling industry for whom he worked—even while aspiring to be one of them. "New Bedford abounds with such Characters who are a set of unfeeling Algerines [pirates] and are not worthy of being called human beings." The exploited sailors "are made outcasts, are trampled upon by Sharks, and despised by those whom they make Rich. They follow the sea, voyage after voyage, and are made dupes by the infernal intrigues of their Employers and outfitters, which eventually brings them to the belief that they are more like Brutes than human beings." He was right: sailors were increasingly exploited in the 1850s, as owners and outfitters became more dependent on "crimps" or "land sharks" to recruit crews. *Harper's* magazine concurred, referring to the "owners of groggeries, boarding-houses, pimps, etc, etc, who trade in the necessities or pander to the vices of the outgoing or returning seamen." An Irish observer left no doubt about the appalling condition of whaling crews: "There is no class of men in the world who are so unfairly dealt with, so oppressed, so degraded, as the seamen who man the vessels engaged in the American whale fishery."[34] These negative developments in the whaling industry would drive Davoll further from the owner class that both attracted and repelled him. "Such men sooner or later will receive their reward," he concluded, "which reward in my opinion will be the inmost recesses of a burning Hell."

Davoll was a man in conflict, distrustful and resentful of the class he aimed to join and identifying with the exploited class, in a slowly dying industry. This downward trend in his chosen profession would continue. The New Bedford whaling trade, just beginning its decline in the mid-1850s, was hard hit during the Civil War (in which twenty-one ships were captured and burned by Confederate raiders) and by Arctic ice disasters in 1871 and 1876 that destroyed thirty local vessels. The last New Bedford whaler, the *Wanderer*, left port in 1924 and was wrecked in a storm just a few miles from the harbor. It's likely that Captain Davoll could have remained in the industry, combining sea voyages with partial ownership, and might have muddled through financially. But his vision of a secure land job, a home, and time with his family was drifting out of reach, and by choosing a seemingly low-risk solution to his dilemma, he ruined his life, severely damaged the family that he was trying to benefit, and helped inflict appalling misery on hundreds of innocent Africans.

If only he had delayed his fateful decision. Just a year later, Davoll's slaving opportunity probably would not have occurred, as arrests and prosecutions increased and slaving agents began leaving the country. Despite the surge in slaving in the 1850s and into the early 1860s, American involvement in the trade finally came to an end, thanks to the Lincoln administration's determination to eradicate it and a change in public opinion in the North during the Civil War. In the 1860 presidential campaign, the Republicans had made the suppression of the slave trade a plank in their party platform: "That we brand the recent reopening of the African slave trade, under the cover of our national flag, aided by perversions of judicial power, as a crime against humanity, a burning shame to our country and age, and we call upon Congress to take prompt and efficient measures for the total and final suppression of that execrable traffic."[35] Once in office, the Lincoln administration took steps to deliver on that promise, particularly in the appointment of district attorneys who would aggressively prosecute slavers. Responding to their success, Secretary of the Interior Caleb Smith wrote, "Much credit is due to the United States attorneys and marshals at New York and Boston for [their] vigilance and zeal." That would include Boston district attorney Richard Henry Dana Jr., who had been relentless in his prosecutions of the *Tahmaroo* and *Margaret Scott* cases.[36]

Increased surveillance in cooperation with the British navy, more arrests (even for merely intending to slave), and more aggressive prosecutions resulted in prison or exile for the agents of the trade. In November 1862, with the arrest of John A. Machado (who had been involved in several of the New Bedford slaving voyages), the *New York Times* could proclaim that "the nest of Slavers in this city is completely broken up."[37] For Americans, the Civil War shattered the indifference that had allowed the slave trade to flourish. African slavery and the slave trade would be finished by the end of the war. Spain finally banned the slave trade to Cuba in 1867, although slavery itself continued there for another quarter century.

The suppression of the slave trade from Africa to the New World was a major humanitarian achievement, yet in the following decades, from 1885 to 1908, the European powers and the United States would look aside as King Leopold of Belgium brutally plundered the Congo of its ivory and rubber and caused the deaths of ten million Africans. This was done in the name of philanthropic improvement for the people of Congo and, in a bitter irony, to extinguish the remnants of the slave trade in Africa.[38]

The disturbing fact remains that there are more people enslaved globally *today* in forced labor, child labor, and human trafficking than there were in 1860.[39] Apparently, the greed, racism, and moral indifference to the suffering of vulnerable people that underlay the African slave trade are still very much with us.

CHAPTER 12

THE CURIOUS CASE OF
THE SHIP *B*_____

O n October 2, 1921, the *New Bedford Sunday Standard* published a full-page story under the headline "On a New
Bedford Slaver in 1860."[1] Written by Pemberton H. Nye, a
prominent local businessman, it purported to relate his experience on the whaler-slaver *"B_____"* under the command of
"Captain D_____," which left port in August 1860 for a whaling voyage that instead sailed to Africa to purchase slaves and
transported them to Cuba. The similarities to Captain Davoll's
1860 voyage on the *Brutus* strongly suggest that Nye was remi-
niscing about this very event.[2]

Pemberton Nye's tale begins in Boston in 1860, when he saw
a poster on Commercial Street, advertising for a whaling crew.
After signing up, Nye was transported by train to New Bedford,
where he and several other men signed their shipping papers
for an eighteen- to twenty-four-month cruise in the North and
South Atlantic and were ferried by "Shark-boat" to their ship.
The revenue cutter *Daring* came up alongside, and an officer
boarded the *B_____* for a brief inspection and then left. As
soon as the ship got out to sea, the crew practiced lowering
boats and other whaling maneuvers. In the Azores they chased
whales several times but never landed any; to Nye's surprise,
the captain didn't seem to care.

Fifty days out they were stopped by a British naval ship off
the coast of Africa, and a lieutenant boarded. After twenty min-
utes in the captain's cabin, the lieutenant came on deck and

inspected the tryworks, and finding the pots unusually clean he asked how much oil they had taken. The captain replied that they had whaled in the Azores but had been unsuccessful because the crew was too green, so he had sailed to the coast of Africa to give them practice hunting humpbacks. The skeptical lieutenant left, predicting he would see them again. The captain was heard to remark to the mate, "Blast his heart. How I should like to sink his old tub and drown every soul on board; he don't want to see a man earn an honest living." The man-of-war sailed on, and they never saw it again.

Later that day a boat rowed up with a Spaniard in charge of an African crew.[3] They boarded, and the captain and the Spaniard greeted each other as old friends and went to the cabin to confer. When they left, the *B_____* cruised the coast for two weeks. The crew had now become very suspicious that this was a slaving voyage but felt helpless since no one but the captain and mate could navigate the ship. As Nye remarked, "The humbug of whaling was now played out."

As they sailed in close to a largely uninhabited stretch of shore, Nye could see a long, low shed on the beach. The captain kept checking with the mate, who had gone aloft, if a sail was visible. "It's strange, he ought to be there," the captain was heard to mutter. Finally, a sail was sighted, and soon a boat pulled up with the Spaniard aboard. Nye could plainly see the shed, which he later learned was called a barracoon. A short while later boats began to approach the ship, "crammed full of naked Negroes." Once the "cargo" was in the hold, "We now hove up and made all sail on the ship, and by seven o'clock the *B_____* with 800 prime Negroes in her hold was on her way to Cuba."

Nye explained how the captives were fed. One of the whaling try-pots was used for cooking. Each slave was given a small tub of rice and a piece of hardtack. If they refused to eat, the Spaniard whipped them with a piece of tarred ratline. After the rice, each slave was given a quart of water to drink. The meal over, the crew disinfected the deck with carbolic acid. Later, Nye and others went below to check on the captives who were packed tightly, with one man's chest touching the back of the next and so filling "the length and width of the hold." "Pent up in such close quarters, and inhaling such a terrible stench, it was miraculous that one half of them had not perished. We found six or seven dead bodies which were at once hauled up on deck and thrown overboard." After four weeks about twenty of the slaves had died, mostly from dysentery.

Nye described how a crew member named Steve became ill and was confined to his berth. The rats had left the crowded hold and now congregated in the forecastle, which drove the crew to sleep and eat on deck. Steve was left "in that dismal hole with no one but the rats to keep him company through the dreary night." He died on the third day and was sewn in canvas weighted with old iron and dropped overboard. The captain did not read the service for burial at sea.

When they approached Cuba, a large number of small boats appeared and began taking the slaves to shore, at a small village called Quitero. The process was very efficient, and all were landed in less than two hours. The B_____ then made for Havana, where all the gear associated with slaving was thrown overboard. The ship was sprinkled with chloride of lime, "but nothing would ever eradicate that terrible odor which clung to the ship." They dropped anchor in Havana Harbor. "If any inconsistencies existed in her papers they were unnoticed at the Custom House," Nye remarked, "as things can be managed very cleverly in Havana, when you knew how."

Nye and the other sailors received $500 in gold for their participation. He heard later that the owners netted $50,000. The ship was sold to a Cuban company and put under the Spanish flag. Nye "hung around Havana for a few weeks" before taking a steamer to New York.

~~~~~~

So ends Pemberton Nye's published account of his unintended involvement in the slave trade in 1860–61. While his narrative (abridged here) provides interesting and believable detail of a slaving voyage—and closely resembles that of the *Brutus*—there are too many discrepancies from other sources, particularly the firsthand testimony of *Brutus* crew member Milo Robbins. In Nye's account, the captain remained on the ship the entire time, which does not match Davoll's departure in the Azores. The *Brutus* was not inspected by the revenue cutter *Daring* in New Bedford Harbor, nor was it boarded by the British navy off the coast of Africa (although it was briefly inspected by the U.S. Navy). According to Nye, the *B*_____ had a slave deck (a platform constructed in the hold specifically to accommodate a large number of slaves), and the slaves were restrained with iron manacles; neither was used in Robbins's account of the *Brutus* voyage.

Twenty slaves died in passage on the *B*_____; on the *Brutus*, at least one hundred perished. The death of Steve in the rat-infested forecastle is a dramatic part of Nye's story, but there was no "Steve" on the *Brutus*, nor did Milo Robbins report any crew deaths aboard ship. Robbins did relate the death of a different sailor, Frederick Standish, but this occurred after they had reached Cuba. Robbins gave a full account of the crew in his court testimony; surely, he would have mentioned the grim passing of Steve.

Furthermore, there was only one Pemberton H. Nye in New Bedford, and he was born in 1870—ten years after the *Brutus* sailed.

What can we make of this extraordinary story, written nearly one hundred years ago and six decades after the *Brutus* voyage? The details—about brutal punishment, slaves discarded overboard, how food was prepared, how slaves were crowded into the hold, the stench, the disinfectant—are very typical of a slaving voyage and add a grim realism to the account. But it turns out that Nye did not take part in this voyage.

He created a composite story, fictionalized for dramatic effect, and much of his material came from another slaving account.

The giveaway is the death of Steve in the forecastle. While there was no Steve on board the *Brutus*, "The Death of Steve" is the title of a chapter of *Six Months on a Slaver,* a narrative published in 1879 by Edward Manning, describing his slaving voyage on the false whaler *Thomas Watson* out of New London, Connecticut, in 1860.[4] Much of Nye's details are directly lifted from Manning's story: the visit by the British naval officer, the description of the barracoons on the African coast, the brutal flogging of a slave, Steve's death and unceremonious burial—even the fact that the Spanish captain had completed eight previous slaving voyages. Nye's account is, in fact, mostly plagiarized.

Nye's story is not reliable enough to be woven into the actual history of the *Brutus*. It is included here because there is some real connection to the voyage, and the details are so compelling that his account can't be ignored. Why Pemberton H. Nye chose to tell this story in 1921, link it to the *Brutus* voyage, plagiarize details from a book published in 1879, and relate it as his own experience is a mystery.

CHAPTER 13

CAPTAIN EDWARD S. DAVOLL
(1822–1863)

It took an extraordinary man to make a career in the perilous business of chasing leviathans over the world's oceans. Yet Edward Davoll was in so many ways an ordinary man, very conventional in his attitudes about marriage, religion, the moral education of his daughter, and other matters. He was conventional in his racial prejudices as well. Today we would consider him racist, but he was probably no more so than the average nineteenth-century American.

What is remarkable is how this ordinary man got caught up in something as extraordinarily evil as the slave trade. He became disillusioned with whaling, as his early career dreams were crushed by diminishing returns, longer voyages, and no apparent way to achieve his desire to be home with his family. But he made some poor decisions as he looked for a way out of his financial problems. There was, despite his Christian pronouncements, a sort of moral emptiness about him. It would be easier to understand a single moment of weakness, but Davoll engaged twice in slaving, on the *Atlantic* in 1859 and the *Brutus* in 1860. He did not actually participate in the dirty business of buying and selling slaves, but he played an indispensable role in fitting out false whalers and lending legitimacy to these operations.

As we come to understand Davoll and the perils and frustrations in his life, he seems less evil than morally weak. Much has been written about the banality of evil: how ordinary people

FIGURE 13. In this undated daguerreotype, Edward Davoll was probably in his late thirties. Courtesy of the New Bedford Whaling Museum.

could play a part in an undertaking of extraordinary iniquity.[1] Like his fellow mariners Skinner, Landre, and Bigelow, Davoll was cowardly, looking for an easy way to make money. If we're looking for evil men, there are the professional slavers like Pierre Pearce, Appleton Oaksmith, and John Machado who made their living in slaving ventures, time and again. It's hard to find redeeming qualities in them. By comparison, Davoll comes across as an innocent of sorts, drawn into the web by clever men who could feed on his dissatisfaction and promise a way out.

Yet he knew what he was doing. Most men would have recoiled from an offer to go slaving. Compare Davoll to the captain and first mate of the Westport whaler *Leonidas:* in 1857, stopping at Kabenda, the captain was offered a cargo of slaves to transport to Brazil. As a crew member explained, "The captain wanted to do so, but Mr. Brown, our mate, said 'No, he had not come slaving.'" Mr. Brown had the moral backbone that Davoll lacked.[2]

We don't know if he felt remorse over what he did. It's likely he regretted that the *Brutus* voyage was found out and that he had been implicated and arrested, but to regret getting caught is different from penitence. He made no public expression of contrition—in fact, he maintained his innocence and did not pay his fine—but maybe he did in private, to his wife. His death cut short any chance of restitution or amends. Had he gone to prison, he might have then begged forgiveness and attempted to rebuild his life and career, but it's likely he would have been shunned by the New Bedford whaling elite, with little chance of regaining his master status. Few of the men who were convicted of slaving did well later in New Bedford.

Edward Davoll believed in an afterlife. He once wrote that the "sharks" who exploited the sailors of New Bedford would eventually be rewarded in the "inmost recesses of a burning Hell." We can only guess at his fate beyond the grave: What justice awaited the believer whose actions contributed to the death or lifetime slavery of more than one thousand Africans?

FIGURE 14. Edward Davoll died on April 15, 1863, and was buried in his home-town of Westport. Later his wife, Elizabeth, and daughter, Carrie, were buried in the same plot. Photo by the author.

CHAPTER 14
CONSEQUENCES

Many people in this story were caught in the extensive web of the transatlantic slave trade, some willingly and some as victims. Here, as best as can be determined, is how their involvement affected the rest of their lives.

After dying of typhoid fever in April 1863, Edward Davoll was buried in the family plot at Linden Grove Cemetery in his hometown of Westport. Chiseled into his headstone is the title "Captain," but there are no details of his life—and certainly no mention of his role in slave trading. Some family members saved his letters, which were purchased by the New Bedford Whaling Museum in 2005.

Edward's parents, Jeremiah and Barbara Davoll, outlived him. At Jeremiah's death in 1875 his estate was worth $4,800, indicating a moderately wealthy family. There is a story that Jeremiah enlisted in the army during the Civil War. If so, it would be a fitting counterpoint to his son's involvement in the slave trade. But Jeremiah was sixty-five when the war began, so the story is unlikely.

Edward's wife, Elizabeth Davoll, joined him at Linden Grove Cemetery nine months later. She died in New Bedford on January 20, 1863, at the age of thirty-four. The official cause of death was consumption, but it's hard not to think heartbreak had something to do with it. How little we know about Elizabeth! Only one of her letters was saved, so we mostly know her through Edward's reactions to hers. She doesn't come through as an individual in her own right. We can fill in based on books about whalers' wives (so well done by Lisa Norling), but Elizabeth was a flesh-and-blood person that we can't quite capture. We can surmise that her life was frustrating, if not downright unhappy, and illness and shame certainly made it worse. Was she aware of her husband's slaving? The New Bedford newspapers suspected, so she could not have been totally ignorant. Perhaps she knew and felt it was worth it to get him home? These are hard questions with no answers.

Elizabeth had endured the usual difficulties of a whaling captain's wife, especially the long absences: for three-quarters of their married life, he was at sea. She had surely expected that at the end of his active career they would settle in a comfortable home like the captains' residences at Westport Point or at least a sufficient retirement with a resident husband. Instead, she had to endure the humiliation of his imprisonment and the distress of his early death.

With the loss of both parents, Carrie Davoll went to live with an aunt and uncle in Westport. We have a document, an undated school essay probably written when she was in her early teens, describing the village at the Head of Westport. Her teacher's comment—"Very fine indeed"—could not have been more at odds with the reality of Carrie's life. Her father had been mostly at sea, and when finally on dry land he was under indictment. She was eight when her father passed away and nine when her mother died in 1863—a year that also featured the slaughter at Gettysburg and other horrors of the Civil War. Carrie worked as a clerk, never married, and died at age thirty-eight of metritis, an inflammation of the uterus. Like her mother, she was to be a beneficiary of Edward Davoll's illegal venture but turned out to be a victim. She is buried with both parents at Linden Grove in Westport.[1]

Albert Bigelow, the sham owner of the *Brutus,* had moved to New Bedford from Rochester, New York, because of a "girl scrape." Sentenced to five years in prison for his role

FIGURE 15. This undated photograph of Carrie Davoll was probably taken when she was in her early thirties. Orphaned as a young child, Carrie worked as a clerk, never married, and died at age thirty-eight. Courtesy of the New Bedford Whaling Museum.

in the slaving voyage, he managed to escape and hid out on Nashawena (one of the Elizabeth Islands off the coast of southeastern Massachusetts, only ten miles by water from New Bedford) with the parents of Captain Jesse T. Sherman. He then went to Hilton Head, North Carolina, where he worked as clerk for a "religious and temperance enthusiast"—curious for a former liquor dealer. We last hear of him in 1900 when he is listed as a pension broker in Washington, DC, and described as "a thin, spry, well-preserved man, with a wife and daughter."[2] Except for being forced to leave New Bedford, Bigelow appears to have suffered little from his engagement in slaving.

New Bedford outfitter Andrew Potter was, like Edward Davoll, originally from Westport. He had been arrested with

Bigelow on suspicion of knowingly outfitting a slaver but was released due to lack of evidence. According to *Representative Men and Old Families of Southeastern Massachusetts,* he was successful in business and lived well, but other sources indicate that he sold his New Bedford business shortly after the *Brutus* affair and died poor. An account of his funeral reads: "Andrew Howard Potter died in 1899, a respected Citizen. Large funeral, attendance of the finest body of men I have seen on any such occasion. Leaving a fine Will and house only—the latter to his widow. Died poor— had had [to] struggle for appearances for years. An odd mixture of ruffian speech and kindly actions, a gentleman as per my treatment and experiences with him, prompt and good pay, etc."[3]

Pierre L. Pearce is one of the villains of the story, a man who played a critical role in the death and enslavement of thousands of Africans. As recounted earlier, he was a ship chandler, with a store on South Street in New York City, and had been the agent behind the purchase of the *Brutus* in Warren, Rhode Island, and its transfer to New York and then to New Bedford, where Albert Bigelow was induced to be the nominal owner. Little is known about Pearce, except that he was part of an international slaving network and that between 1857 and 1860 he and his associates were middlemen in the purchase of at least fifty-six ships (for owners mostly in Cuba) to be used in the slave trade. When Pearce and Bigelow were arrested and taken to Boston, Pearce posted $10,000 bail, which he forfeited when he absconded. Most reports suggest he left the country. Since he is known to have spent two months in Havana in 1861, he most likely made his way there when the American authorities were closing in on him in 1862.[4]

Another accomplice recruited by Pearce was First Mate William H. Jackson, of Portsmouth, Rhode Island. He took command of the *Brutus* when Davoll, as planned, left the ship in the Azores. After delivering his cargo of slaves, Jackson remained in Cuba with two other crew members and apparently continued slaving (possibly on the *Brutus*). Like Pearce and Bigelow, he never paid a price for his involvement in the slave trade.[5]

Standing in stark contrast to these criminals are Milo Robbins and Jerome Colburn, two young men from Belchertown, Massachusetts, who unwittingly signed up for a legitimate whaling voyage on the *Brutus,* only to find themselves on a slaver. Both had the courage to testify to federal authorities and newspapers about the slaving operation and were instrumental in the indictments of Davoll, Bigelow, and Pearce. Robbins spent nearly nine months in a Boston jail as a witness, for which he was paid one dollar per day. Listed in the census as a twenty-year-old married farmer in 1863, he enlisted in the Twenty-First Massachusetts Infantry. We don't know what happened to him after that.

Colburn hoped that military service in the Civil War would atone for his (unwilling) participation in the slave trade. A local newspaper described his situation in 1861: "Young Colburn returned home recently with his share of sale of $1.00 for each slave. He does not feel that he is to blame for his part in the enterprise, as he was totally ignorant of the character of the vessel, and would have escaped if he could." In June 1861 Colburn enlisted in the U.S. Navy. Within two years he was dead of consumption.[6]

Long before his involvement with the whaler-slaver *Margaret Scott* in New Bedford, Appleton Oaksmith had run guns to Cuba, acted as minister to the United States for the illegal government set up in Nicaragua by William Walker, and been implicated in at least two slave-trading voyages. Finally caught in the *Margaret Scott* affair, Oaksmith was convicted on eight counts, but while awaiting sentencing he escaped (apparently, the jail was being repaired, and he walked out disguised as a workman). Oaksmith made his way to Maine and then to England, from where he ran guns to the Confederacy during the Civil War. Later, disguised as his own lawyer, he had the audacity to gain an audience with President Ulysses S. Grant to plead for a pardon—and succeeded. He lived out the remainder of his life as a plantation owner, railroad president, and financial schemer in North Carolina. He was certainly a colorful character—but a criminal whose actions resulted in the deaths of countless Africans.[7]

Ambrose S. Landre was forty-seven, with a wife, son, young daughter, and a newborn, when he was recruited by Oaksmith to take command of the *Margaret Scott*. He had once been a captain but lost his master-mariner status and was easy prey for Oaksmith and his money. Compounding his dreadful decision to engage in slaving, he brought his nineteen-year-old son into the illicit venture. Landre appears to have received a reduced sentence for his role as a government witness. His son, Ambrose W. Landre, had also been indicted, but seems to have served no jail time, as he shows up as a crew member on the whaler *Corinthian* in 1862. Landre Sr. remained in New Bedford and somehow retained his standing as a master mariner. In 1870 his real and personal property were valued at $2,000, so he apparently found his financial footing after his disgrace, possibly due to the fact that he cooperated in the prosecution of Oaksmith.[8]

Samuel Skinner was induced by Oaksmith and Landre to act as sham owner of the *Margaret Scott,* and for that he was convicted of engaging in the slave trade and sentenced to five years in prison. He was released after two years, having been pardoned by President Abraham Lincoln, but debtor's court records indicate that his financial problems continued. After the *Margaret Scott* was seized and sold, Skinner (as former owner) sued for reimbursement. Not surprisingly, he lost. By 1865 he had left New Bedford and was living in Boston with his wife, Lydia, and listed as a "mariner." He died of consumption at East Boston in 1875 at the age of sixty-eight and was buried—as he was born—on Nantucket.[9]

New Bedford jewelry-shop owner Zeno Kelley was the official owner of the false whaler *Tahmaroo*. Although the voyage failed to deliver any slaves, Kelley was arrested and tried for fitting out a ship with the intent to engage in the slave trade. His co-conspirators, Captain Jabez S. Hathaway, replacement captain John C. Cook, and First Mate Luther Whittemore, all left the country to avoid prosecution. Cook was later captured and turned state's evidence; Kelley was found guilty and sentenced to four years in jail and a fine of $1,000.

Kelley had influential friends in New Bedford who petitioned President Lincoln for a pardon, based on Kelley's continued insistence of innocence. Lincoln did grant a pardon, but while it was being processed through the State Department new evidence emerged of Kelley's further crimes while in prison.

After Lincoln's assassination, Kelley's supporters petitioned President Andrew Johnson for a pardon, claiming he had acted "in a moment of weakness, at the instigation of others." As detailed in chapter 10, Massachusetts District Attorney Richard Henry Dana Jr. fought all efforts to pardon Kelley because of his continued illegal activities while in prison, including witness tampering and blackmailing his financial backers in New Bedford. After serving three years of his four-year sentence, Kelley finally did receive a pardon and returned to New Bedford. But his finances and reputation were in ruins, and he died two years later of "congestion of the brain," at age forty-five.[10]

His partner in crime Jabez Hathaway was indicted twice, but was never convicted. A rumor circulated that he hid in the attic of his house in New Bedford for three years to escape prosecution. In any event, he remained in the city but like Kelley spent time in debtor's court. He died in 1883.[11]

There are few heroes in this story, but Richard Henry Dana Jr. is certainly one. As district attorney for Massachusetts in the *Tahmaroo* (and many other) slaving trials, he was relentless in the prosecution of slave traders and their allies. It was Dana who kept digging up incriminating evidence that kept Zeno Kelley in jail for most of his sentence. In that case, Dana worked closely with a Hawaiian crew member of the *Tahmaroo* who provided crucial evidence. His experience with and appreciation of Hawaiian seamen, as related in his popular book *Two Years before the Mast*, proved critical in that case. A great admirer of Abraham Lincoln, Dana resigned from his position as district attorney in 1866 because of differences with the Johnson administration. Dana's commitment to antislavery and his habit of giving free legal advice to indigent sailors put him at odds with Boston's Brahmin leaders, who considered him a traitor to his class. His heartfelt concern for the poor and oppressed combined with a fine legal mind played an important part in the suppression of the African slave trade from American ports.[12]

Two of the background figures in the worldwide slaving network were John A. Machado and Mary Jane Watson. A naturalized U.S. citizen originally from Portugal, Machado disguised his slaving through his legitimate trading in African palm oil. He was involved in the false whalers *Atlantic, Brutus, Margaret Scott,* and *Tahmaroo* and reportedly had outfitted more than half the slavers out of New York City between 1856 and 1861. The *New York Times* called him the "king of the slave-traders in this city."[13] Machado was supremely confident: when one of his slave ships was captured by the Royal Navy, he had the nerve to sue the British government for $80,000 for interfering with his legitimate business trading with Africa. Arrested at least three times, Machado managed to avoid prison and died in Brooklyn of Bright's disease in 1894.[14] Like so many agents of the slave trade, he managed to remain elusive while smaller and less clever players were caught and prosecuted.

Such was not the case for his partner and paramour, Mary Jane Watson. Described by a New York newspaper as a "dashing and very stylish female," Watson was a ruthless agent in the slave trade. (While the slave trade was considered a "masculine" endeavor, as many as forty-eight women took part in the slave trade between 1656 and 1863.) Implicated in three slaving voyages, and facing indictment in New York in 1862, Watson escaped to Spain, only to find the U.S. consul blocking her slaving activity at Cádiz. She took to drink and, according to the *New York Times,* "soon terminated her existence by the bottle." So few of the slave traders were punished, we can take some satisfaction that Mrs. Watson's life ended in misery, a fitting finale to a career of exploiting innocent people.[15]

What became of the ship *Brutus?* There were a variety of reports: that it had been burned after delivering its cargo of slaves to Cuba in 1861, or sold to parties in Cuba and its name changed, or abandoned and left to break up in the surf. Any of these are possible, since slaving vessels were often destroyed or sold to remove any evidence of the trade. The most likely outcome is that it was sold and under a different name made several more voyages out of Cuba until 1864, when it was burned. It is possible that William Jackson, the first mate under Captain Davoll, was in command as he continued his slaving career out of Cuba.[16]

After the capture of the *Margaret Scott,* the *New Bedford Republican Standard* reported: "The *Margaret Scott,* by order of the Court, has been sold, the U.S. government becoming the purchaser. She will help stop up a slave port, instead of engaging in the slave trade." This was a reference to the Stone Fleet. In order to blockade Southern ports in the first year of the Civil War, the U.S. Navy purchased thirty ships (seventeen of them New Bedford whalers), filled them with seventy-five hundred tons of local stone, and scuttled them in Charleston Harbor, South Carolina, in December 1861 and January 1862. It was a military failure: the ships settled into the sandy bottom or broke up, and soon the channels were navigable again. As the local story goes, the only beneficiaries seem to have been

FIGURE 16. The Stone Fleet, *Harper's* magazine, January 11, 1862. In the winter of 1861–62, the Union navy sent thirty old ships to Charleston, South Carolina, in an unsuccessful attempt to block the harbor. Seventeen of the ships were derelict whalers, including the would-be slaver *Margaret Scott*. Courtesy of the New Bedford Whaling Museum.

the New Bedford–area farmers, who finally made money from the stones growing in their fields.[17]

Five hundred African men, women, and children were transported on the *Brutus* and sold into slavery to work the sugar plantations of Cuba. And there were so many others: the *New York Times* estimated in 1862 that thirty thousand slaves had been landed in Cuba just in the year between November 1859 and November 1860. Their existence was brutal and short, with life expectancy estimated at eight years after arrival, suggesting that most of the five hundred slaves transported on the *Brutus* in 1861 were probably dead by the time Cuban slavery ended in 1886.[18] These people should be at the very center of a story of the slave trade, but for the *Brutus* voyage—and most others—we have no names, just numbers and reports of brutality and death. Their marginalization has been very upsetting during the writing of this book. A good fiction writer could have imagined lives for them and illuminated their suffering and their humanity, but this is a work of history and the records are silent.

NOTES

ABBREVIATIONS

All references to the newspaper *Whalemen's Shipping List* (hereafter abbreviated *WSL*) were retrieved from the Mystic Seaport website, https://research.mysticseaport.org/reference/whalemens-shipping-list.

All letters to and from Captain Edward Davoll (abbreviated ESD) are in the Davoll Family Papers at the New Bedford Whaling Museum (NBWM).

The Old Dartmouth Historical Society (ODHS) is part of the New Bedford Whaling Museum.

Much of the genealogical information, such as birth, death, wills, and probate, comes from various public sources, retrieved through Ancestry.com.

A NOTE ON THE TRANSATLANTIC SLAVE TRADE

1. David Eltis and David Richardson, *Atlas of the Transatlantic Slave Trade* (New Haven, CT: Yale University Press, 2010), 307; David Brion Davis, *Inhuman Bondage: The Rise and Fall of Slavery in the New World* (New York: Oxford University Press, 2006), 37–38. Direct trade from Africa to the Americas began in 1525. While most of the African slaves were transported from West Africa, about 4.3 percent came from the southeastern coast and Madagascar. Eltis and Richardson, *Atlas*, xxiv, 15.

2. Dale W. Tomich, *The Politics of the Second Slavery* (Albany: SUNY Press, 2016), 6–7; David Eltis and David Richardson, "The Transatlantic Slave Trade and the Civil War," *New York Times,* January 13, 2011; Karl Marx, *Capital: A Critique of Political Economy* (London: Penguin Classics, 1990), 915.

3. Eltis and Richardson, *Atlas*, 2.

4. The various acts to regulate the slave trade are covered thoroughly in "The Abolition of the Slave Trade," New York Public Library, http://abolition.nypl.org.

5. Leonardo Marques, *The United States and the Transatlantic Slave Trade to the Americas, 1776–1867* (New Haven, CT: Yale University Press, 2016), 187.

6. W. E. B. Du Bois, *The Suppression of the African Slave-Trade to the United States of America* (1896; reprint, New York: Oxford University Press, 2007), 112; Marques, *Transatlantic Slave Trade*, 258; Eltis and Richardson, *Atlas*, 303.

CHAPTER 1: A WHALING CAREER

1. The original Indian names for the rivers have been replaced by the more prosaic names East and West Branches of the Westport River.

2. This information comes from the 1850 census, as earlier censuses do not provide much detail about farming.

3. Donald R. Walters, "Ruby Devol Finch: Recent Discoveries," *Antiques and Fine Art Magazine*, www.afanews.com.

4. *Early Schooldays in Westport*, Westport Historical Society.

5. "Whales and Hunting," NBWM, www.whalingmuseum.org.

6. "List of American Whaling Ports, 1784–1926," http://research.mysticseaport.org. Ranked by number of whaling vessels, Westport is fourteenth, a reflection of the smaller ships and shorter voyages out of this lesser port.

7. Martha S. Putney, "Pardon Cook, Whaling Master," *Journal of the Afro-American Historical and Genealogical Society* 4, no. 2 (1983): 52; Stuart Frank, "False Whalers and the Slave Trade," *Seaport* 39, no. 1 (2004). African American and Native American mariners were not uncommon in Westport, as attested by the successful careers of Paul Cuffe and his Wainer in-laws. See Lamont D. Thomas, *Paul Cuffe: Black Entrepreneur and Pan-Africanist* (Urbana: University of Illinois Press, 1988).

8. Alexander Starbuck, *History of the American Whale Fishery* (1878; reprint, Secaucus, NJ: Castle Books, 1989), 364–70.

9. J. Ross Browne, *Etchings of a Whaling Cruise* (New York: Harper & Brothers, 1846), 24.

10. Richard Henry Dana Jr., *Two Years before the Mast* (n.p.: CreateSpace, 2015), 6.

11. Herman Melville, *Moby-Dick* (Evanston, IL: Northwestern University Press, 1988), 159.

12. Briton Cooper Busch, *Whaling Will Never Do for Me: The American Whaleman in the Nineteenth Century* (Lexington: University Press of Kentucky, 1994), 2–3.

13. "Life Aboard," NBWM, www.whalingmuseum.org.

14. Log of the Brig *Elizabeth* (1840), ODHS #745, reel 300, NBWM.

15. Starbuck, *Whale Fishery,* 370–71, 379; Dennis Wood Abstracts, 1:148, NBWM. The rough estimate of Davoll's earnings is based on the calculation of 150 barrels (4,725 gallons) of sperm oil selling at an average price of $1 per gallon in 1840 (Starbuck, *Whale Fishery,* 660), for a total value of catch of $4,725. Using the common rule that the crew received about one-third of the total ($1,575), Davoll's one-sixtieth lay would have amounted to $26. My thanks to whaling historian Michael Dyer of the New Bedford Whaling Museum for reviewing my calculations.

16. Whaleman's Shipping Papers for Brig *Mexico,* Cory Papers, NBWM.

17. Captain Gideon H. Smith to Captain Gideon Davis, April 17 and February 7, 1842, Cory Papers, NBWM.

18. Average prices reported in Starbuck, *Whale Fishery,* 660.

19. Clifford W. Ashley, *The Yankee Whaler* (1926; reprint, New York: Dover, 1991), 102.

20. Elmo P. Hohman, *The American Whaleman* (New York: Longmans, Green, 1928), 41.

21. Earl F. Mulderink III, *New Bedford's Civil War* (New York: Fordham University Press, 2012), 11.

22. Old Dartmouth Historical Sketch, no. 44, NBWM, www.whalingmuseum.org.

23. Busch, *Whaling Will Never Do for Me,* 16.

24. Even under temperance captains, crew members often managed to smuggle alcohol aboard. Ibid., 15.

25. Ibid., 160.

26. *WSL,* April 29, 1845.

27. The calculations are based on average percentage of total value of catch for each rank on New Bedford whaling voyages between 1840 and 1858, in Lance E. Davis, Robert E. Gallman, and Karin Gleiter, "In Pursuit of Leviathan: Technology, Institutions, Productivity, and Profits in American Whaling, 1816–1906," NBER paper (University of Chicago, 1997), 169.

28. *WSL*, September 29, 1846.

29. *WSL*, December 28, 1847, April 25, May 30, and August 1, 1848; Dennis Wood Abstracts, 2:104, NBWM.

30. William C. Davol [*sic*] to ESD, May 14, 1847.

31. *WSL*, November 30, 1847.

CHAPTER 2: CAPTAIN

1. Lisa Norling, *Captain Ahab Had a Wife: New England Women and the Whalefishery, 1720–1870* (Chapel Hill: University of North Carolina Press, 2000), 12; Margaret S. Creighton, *Rights and Passages: The Experience of American Whaling, 1830–1870* (New York: Cambridge University Press, 1995), 42.

2. Starbuck had made captain at age twenty-four and can be seen as a model for how the ambitious Davoll hoped his career would develop. Nathaniel Philbrick, *Away Off Shore: Nantucket Island and Its People, 1602–1890* (New York: Penguin, 2011), 189. Average wages for captains from Lance E. Davis, Robert E. Gallman, and Karin Gleiter, "In Pursuit of Leviathan: Technology, Institutions, Productivity, and Profits in American Whaling, 1816–1906," NBER paper (University of Chicago, 1997), 22.

3. Earl F. Mulderink III, *New Bedford's Civil War* (New York: Fordham University Press, 2012), 15.

4. Davis, Gallman, and Gleiter, "In Pursuit of Leviathan," table 10A.1.

5. Hathaway & Luce (agents) to Captain Henry Manter, March 4, 1849, Martha's Vineyard Museum.

6. Eric Jay Dolin, *Leviathan: The History of Whaling in America* (New York: W. W. Norton, 2007), 211–12.

7. *WSL*, July 31 and October 30, 1849, and June 25, 1850.

8. Davoll's undated orders to his crew were donated to the New Bedford Whaling Museum. The director at that time, Richard C. Kugler, considered the document so valuable that he had it published as a booklet titled *The Captain's Specific Orders* (1981). I am greatly indebted to the late Dick Kugler for sparking my interest in Edward Davoll.

9. ESD to Elizabeth Davoll, May 4, 1851.

10. Alexander Starbuck, *History of the American Whale Fishery* (1878; reprint, Secaucus, NJ: Castle Books, 1989), 114.

11. Davoll purchased two of the sixteen shares in the vessel. *Ship Registers of New Bedford, Massachusetts* (Boston: National Archives Project, 1940), 2:58.

CHAPTER 3: THE PARTING

1. Poem reprinted in Lisa Norling, *Captain Ahab Had a Wife: New England Women and the Whalefishery, 1720–1870* (Chapel Hill: University of North Carolina Press, 2000), 209.

2. Statistics compiled from data in Alexander Starbuck, *History of the American Whale Fishery* (1878; reprint, Secaucus, NJ: Castle Books, 1989), 466–70.

CHAPTER 4: "KEEP A HIGH TOE NAIL & A STIFF UPPER LIP"

1. ESD to Elizabeth Brownell, August 16, 1848.

2. Not only would a North Pacific voyage have been longer, but it would likely have been less successful. In late 1851 the *Whalemen's Shipping List* noted that the reports from the North Pacific were "gloomy and discouraging, and indicate almost a total failure of the fleet." Ships were averaging only 300 barrels of oil, while the average for the previous year was 1,692 barrels. *WSL*, November 25, 1851, and January 13, 1852.

3. Lisa Norling, *Captain Ahab Had a Wife: New England Women and the Whalefishery, 1720–1870* (Chapel Hill: University of North Carolina Press, 2000), 212.

4. *WSL*, November 26, 1850; ESD to Elizabeth Davoll, January 4, 1851.

5. Lemuel Kollock to ESD, April 6, 1851.

6. ESD to Elizabeth Davoll, May 4, 1851.

7. Abbie Dexter Hicks diary, NBWM.

8. ESD to Elizabeth Davoll, May 4, 1851.

9. Ibid.

10. H. Russell to ESD, April 2, 1851.

11. ESD to Elizabeth Davoll, May 26, 1851.

12. *WSL*, February 5, May 4, and June 24, 1851; ESD to Elizabeth Davoll, July 31, 1851. Sailors were so desperate for love letters that the holder of a good one could sell it to lonely crewmates. Margaret S. Creighton, *Rites and Passages: The Experience of American Whaling, 1830–1870* (New York: Cambridge University Press, 1995), 172.

13. Davoll was not alone in wishing he had joined the California Gold Rush. A headline in the New Bedford whaling newspaper announced that "the Reports of the abundance of gold are said to be fully corroborated," and in January 1850 the newspaper printed a list of 131 men from the neighboring town of Dartmouth who were on their way to California. *WSL*, July 31, 1849, and January 29, 1850.

14. ESD to Elizabeth Davoll, July 31, 1851. Delano was dismissed and sent back to New Bedford.

15. ESD to Elizabeth Davoll, September 13, 1851.

16. ESD to Elizabeth Davoll, September 22, 1852.

17. ESD to Elizabeth Davoll, March 26, 1853.

18. ESD to Elizabeth Davoll, January 30, 1852; *Massachusetts Death Records, 1841–1915; Massachusetts Wills and Probate Records*, vols. 96–97, 1851–52.

19. In the 1850s, the average whaling captain's income was ninety dollars per month, so Davoll is just a bit above average on this voyage. Income information is from Lance E. Davis, Robert E. Gallman, and Karin Gleiter, "In Pursuit of Leviathan: Technology, Institutions, Productivity, and Profits in American Whaling, 1816–1906," NBER paper (University of Chicago, 1997). There were nine owners of the *Cornelia* on the 1850 voyage. Davoll's two-sixteenths share was the same as that of Lemuel Kollock, the managing owner, or agent. *Ship Registers of New Bedford, Massachusetts*, vol. 1, *1796–1850* (Boston: National Archives Project, 1940).

20. ESD to Elizabeth Davoll, January 30, 1852.

21. *WSL*, March 15 and July 27, 1852.

22. The quote from the log of the *Wave* is in Briton Cooper Busch, *Whaling Will Never Do for Me: The American Whaleman in the Nineteenth Century* (Lexington: University Press of Kentucky, 2009), 143.

23. Davoll's report was printed in *WSL*, August 3, 1852.

24. ESD to Elizabeth Davoll, March 26, 1852.

25. ESD to Elizabeth Davoll, June 7, 1852.

26. Elizabeth might have been a bit premature in expecting a place of her own. As Lisa Norling writes, "Though whalemen typically married when they had access to income they thought sufficient to begin a family, it appears that their wives rarely maintained an independent household until they had reached midlife, until they had several children, or until they achieved the financial capability to support a separate establishment during the husband's absence." Norling, *Captain Ahab Had a Wife*, 226.

27. *WSL*, September 28 and December 28, 1852, and May 3, 1853; Alexander Starbuck, *History of the American Whale Fishery* (1878; reprint, Secaucus, NJ: Castle Books, 1989), 660.

28. As noted previously, when reliable financial data for a voyage has not been available, I have relied on a useful table of average lay and average percentage of the value of the catch for various ranks on whaling voyages from 1840 to 1858 in Davis, Gallman, and Gleiter, "In Pursuit of Leviathan," 169.

29. Ibid., 390.

30. ESD to Elizabeth Davoll, January 30, 1852.

CHAPTER 5: THE WRECK OF THE *IRIS*

1. ESD to Elizabeth Davoll, August 22, 1854.

2. ESD to Elizabeth Davoll, August 23, 1854.

3. ESD to Elizabeth Davoll, September 28, 1854.

4. The original Portuguese name for the cape was Cabo das Tormentas, or Cape of Storms. After Bartolomeu Dias managed to sail past it to enter the Indian Ocean in 1488, it was renamed Cabo da Boa Esperança. It may have been an overly hopeful name, as Dias was lost at sea during a later expedition around the cape. South Africa History Online, www.sahistory.org.za.

5. *WSL*, October 31, 1854, March 27, and July 31, 1855.

6. ESD to Elizabeth Davoll, March 5, 1855.

7. Lisa Norling examines the role of captains' wives as surrogates for their husbands in business matters in *Ahab Had a Wife: New England Women and the Whale Fishery, 1720–1870* (Chapel Hill: University of North Carolina Press, 2000), 148–49.

8. ESD to Elizabeth Davoll, March 5, 1855.

9. Nina Baym, *Woman's Fiction: A Guide to Novels by and about Women in America, 1820–70* (Urbana: University of Illinois Press, 1993), 151–56.

10. ESD to Elizabeth Davoll, April 25, 1855 (erroneously dated 1854).

11. Norling, *Ahab Had a Wife*, 6–7.

12. ESD to Elizabeth Davoll, March 25, 1855.

13. *WSL*, October 23, 1855.

14. Shipwreck Databases, Western Australian Museum, http://museum.wa.gov.au.

15. *WSL*, October 23, 1855; William Burges to the Colonial Secretary, July 13, 1855, Shipwreck Databases, Western Australian Museum, http://museum.wa.gov.au.

16. Davoll had insured his portion of the oil through Westport businessman C. A. Church and would later ask Church to contact the insurance company for payment. The captain's share was likely one-fifteenth, or ten barrels, with a gross value of about $450. Alexander Starbuck, *History of the American Whale Fishery* (1878; reprint, Secaucus, NJ: Castle Books, 1989), 660.

17. Shipwreck Databases, Western Australian Museum, http://museum.wa.gov.au, particularly the letter from William Burges, the resident magistrate, to the colonial secretary, dated July 13, 1855.

18. Burges to ESD, n.d., ibid.

19. ESD to Elizabeth Davoll, August 20, 1855.

20. Norling, *Captain Ahab Had a Wife*, 123.

21. ESD to Elizabeth Davoll, August 6, 1855.

22. See Reid Mortensen, "Slaving in Australian Courts: Blackbirding Cases, 1869–1871," *Journal of South Pacific Law* 13, no. 1 (2009).

23. ESD to Elizabeth Davoll, December 20, 1855.

24. H. Russell to Elizabeth Davoll, May 14, 1856; ESD to Elizabeth Davoll, December 20, 1855. He did have a few hundred dollars owed him for his share of the *Iris*'s oil, plus other income still coming in from previous voyages and from his share of the *Cornelia*'s profits. Information on the *Wide Awake* is in Glenn A. Knoblock, *The American Clipper Ship, 1845–1920: A Comprehensive History* (Jefferson, NC: McFarland, 2014), 342.

CHAPTER 6: RECOVERY

1. "Reference Book for Elizabeth S. Davoll by Edward S. Davoll, Aug 1856," Davoll Family Papers, NBWM.

2. Lisa Norling, *Captain Ahab Had a Wife: New England Women and the Whale Fishery, 1720–1870* (Chapel Hill: University of North Carolina Press, 2000), 161–62.

3. ESD to C. A. Church, August 1856, NBWM.

4. Lance E. Davis, Robert E. Gallman, and Karin Gleiter, "Agents, Captains, and Owners," in "In Pursuit of Leviathan: Technology, Institutions, Productivity, and Profits in American Whaling, 1816–1906," NBER paper (University of Chicago, 1997).

5. All eight voyages of the *R. L. Barstow* were in the Atlantic, except for its last, which went to the Pacific in 1868. American Offshore Whaling Voyages, https://nmdl.org/projects/aowv/aowv.

6. George's wife, Jane M. Davoll, was English; they met on the island of St. Helena, apparently on one of George's whaling voyages. Unlike his older brother, George owned a home and left an estate of $1,676. *Massachusetts Death Records, 1841–1915; Massachusetts Wills and Probate Records, 1635–1991.*

7. WSL, August 26, 1856. In 1860 Consul Kimball was instrumental in acquiring from the French government a stone from Napoleon's tomb to be part of the Washington Monument, then under construction in Washington, DC. *New York Times,* March 3, 1860. The desertion and discharge are noted in the log of the *R. L. Barstow,* NBWM.

8. Log of the *R. L. Barstow,* NBWM.

9. *WSL*, December 29, 1857; log of the *R. L. Barstow*, NBWM.

10. *WSL*, May 25, 1858. Davoll's letter is in the *R. L. Barstow* log.

11. ESD to Rogers L. Barstow, May 24, 1858.

12. *WSL*, September 7, 1858; Alexander Starbuck, *History of the American Whale Fishery* (1878; reprint, Secaucus, NJ: Castle Books, 1989), 660.

13. *R. L. Barstow* logbook entries, May 31 and June 2, 1859.

14. *WSL*, October 25, 1859.

15. Davis, Gallman, and Gleiter, "In Pursuit of Leviathan," 173.

16. Not surprisingly, the equivalent French expression, "filer à l'Anglaise," translates to "English leave." *Oxford English Dictionary*.

17. *WSL*, July 12, 1860.

18. *New Bedford Standard*, July 31, 1860; E. M. Archibald to Lord Lyons, February 1, 1861, *Accounts and Papers of the House of Commons* (1862), 61:157–58. Archibald's letter claims that Davoll had already been involved with the *Atlantic*, as he had "gone out in her"—that is, from New Bedford. This could be true, but there is no corroborating evidence.

19. Log of the ship *Atlantic*, NBWM.

20. Archibald to Lyons, February 1, 1861, *Parliamentary Papers*, 157–58.

21. Ibid.; Leonardo Marques, *The United States and the Transatlantic Slave Trade to the Americas, 1776–1867* (New Haven, CT: Yale University Press, 2016), 204.

CHAPTER 7: "WHAT'S IN THE WIND?"

1. Jonathan Bourne Papers, ms. 18, NBWM. On the wreck of the *Dolphin*, see *WSL*, January 24, 1860. The *Dolphin* had been insured for $24,000, but like most whaling voyages it was probably underinsured.

2. *WSL*, July 24 and August 14, 1860.

3. Charles Walter Agard Collection, ms. 23, NBWM.

4. Leonardo Marques, *The United States and the Transatlantic Slave Trade to the Americas, 1776–1867* (New Haven, CT: Yale University Press, 2016), 189. Pierre Pearce was involved in as many as fifty-six slaving voyages between 1857 and 1860, mostly to Cuba. See Ted Maris-Wolf, "Of Blood and Treasure: Recaptive Africans and the Politics of Slave Trade Suppression," *Journal of the Civil War Era* 4, no. 1 (2014): 54. The *Brutus* was sold at auction to Edsall & Webb, a company of shipwrights, caulkers, and sparmakers on South Street in New York City, who could have been acting as intermediaries for Pearce. So R. B. Johnson, who had just

lost the *Dolphin* in a shipwreck in 1859, might have wanted to unload his last whaler and had no idea it was intended for slaving. Walter Nebiker whaling notes, Warren (RI) Preservation Society; *Trow's New York City Directory* (New York, 1865), 87.

5. Unspecified New Bedford newspaper, September 25, 1861, Agard Collection, NBWM.

6. *WSL*, August 21, 1860.

7. *WSL*, August 28, 1860.

8. Unidentified New Bedford newspaper, August 18, 1860, Agard Collection, NBWM.

9. *New York Times*, November 17, 1862; Dale W. Tomich, *Through the Prism of Slavery: Labor, Capital, and World Economy* (Lanham, MD: Rowman & Littlefield, 2003), 75.

10. *New York Times*, November 17, 1862.

11. Warren S. Howard, *American Slavers and the Federal Law* (Berkeley: University of California Press, 1963), 236–37; Lance E. Davis, Robert E. Gallman, and Karin Gleiter, "In Pursuit of Leviathan: Technology, Institutions, Productivity, and Profits in American Whaling, 1816–1906," NBER paper (University of Chicago, 1997), table 11.2.

12. When Adams was secretary of state, asked by the British foreign minister if anything was worse than the slave trade, Adams replied, "Yes. Admitting the right of search by foreign officers of our vessels upon the seas in time of peace; for that would be making slaves of ourselves." David Waldstreicher and Matthew Mason, *John Quincy Adams and the Politics of Slavery* (New York: Oxford University Press, 2016), 103.

13. *New York World*, August 29, 1860, quoted in Agard Collection, NBWM; registry information in *Ship Registers of New Bedford, Massachusetts*, vol. 2 (Boston: National Archives Project, 1940). The Revenue Service had been alerted by New York authorities during the attempt to outfit the *Brutus* in New York. It was because of this scrutiny that Pearce decided to transfer ownership to a willing New Bedford sham owner, which now focused suspicion on New Bedford. See Agard Collection, NBWM.

14. *New York World*, August 29, 1860; *WSL*, September 4, 1860; Agard Collection, NBWM.

15. "Testimony of a Hand on Board the Ship Brutus," *Boston Journal*, August 21, 1861; Agard Collection, NBWM. There is no record of how Chase and Pierce fared.

16. Agard Collection, NBWM; Stuart M. Frank, "False Whalers and the Slave Trade," *Seaport* (WinterSpring 2004): 22.

17. Howard, *American Slavers and the Federal Law*, 238.

18. Needless to say, records of a slaving voyage were rarely kept, so aside from the February 14 departure from Africa, there is very little information about the chronology of the *Brutus* voyage.

19. "Testimony of a Hand on Board the Ship Brutus"; Agard Collection, box 3, folder 7, "Ship Brutus," NBWM.

20. *U.S. v. Pierre Pearce,* National Archives, Waltham, MA.

21. Unidentified newspaper account, August 9, 1861, quoted in Agard Collection, NBWM.

22. Howard, *American Slavers and the Federal Law,* 233.

23. Agard Collection, NBWM.

24. *New York Times,* August 22, 1861; Agard Collection, NBWM.

25. Undated New Bedford newspaper editorial, August or September 1861, Agard Collection, NBWM.

CHAPTER 8: EVASION

1. "American Offshore Whaling Voyages," National Maritime Digital Library, https://nmdl.org; *Ship Registers of New Bedford, Massachusetts,* vol. 2 (Boston: National Archives Project, 1940). When the *Palmyra* was sold in 1856, the price was $2,800 (*WSL,* June 3, 1856), which provides some indication of its value in 1861.

2. It is not surprising that the *Palmyra* was withdrawn from whaling in 1862 and used in the more suitable coasting trade. Alexander Starbuck, *History of the American Whale Fishery* (1878; reprint, Secaucus, NJ: Castle Books, 1989), 583.

3. Logbook of the ship *Atlantic,* with partial log of the schooner *Palmyra,* August 9–November 11, 1861, NBWM.

4. Log of the *Palmyra,* August 11, 1861, NBWM; *WSL,* April 30, 1861; ESD to Elizabeth Davoll, June 30, 1861.

5. *New York Times,* May 31, 1863.

6. Log of the *Palmyra,* September 4, 1861, NBWM.

7. Briton Cooper Busch, *Whaling Will Never Do for Me: The American Whaleman in the Nineteenth Century* (Lexington: University Press of Kentucky, 2009), 31.

8. *WSL,* June 8, 1852.

9. Log of ship *Parachute* of New Bedford, 1857, quoted in Busch, *Whaling Will Never Do for Me,* 30.

10. ESD to Elizabeth Davoll, May 26 and September 13, 1851.

11. "Character of Officers and Crew," log of the *R. L. Barstow,* NBW 1251 A and B, NBWM.

12. *WSL,* December 23, 1856.

13. *Palmyra* log, September 5 and September 30, 1861.

14. *Palmyra* log, October 17, 1861. The bomb lance was a harpoon with an explosive head launched from a shoulder-fired gun. Introduced in the 1850s, it was much more effective than the traditional harpoon hurled by the boatsteerer. Some of these lances exploded on contact, killing or mortally wounding the whale. "Whales and Hunting," NBWM, www.whalingmuseum.org. A "gullied" whale is one that has become excited or frightened. William F. Macy and Roland B. Hussey, eds., *The Nantucket Scrap Basket: Being a Collection of Characteristic Stories and Sayings of the People of the Town and Island of Nantucket* (Nantucket, MA: Inquirer and Mirror Press, 1916), 17.

15. *Palmyra* log, October 11, November 7, and November 17, 1861. There was only one lighthouse at Bermuda at the time, the Gibbs' Hill Lighthouse (built in 1846) on the Southampton coast.

16. *Palmyra* log, November 16 and November 21, 1861.

17. ESD to Elizabeth Davoll, November 21, 1861.

18. Catherine Lynch Deichmann, *Rogues and Runners: Bermuda and the American Civil War* (Hamilton: Bermuda National Trust, 2003), 60.

19. N. Gifford to ESD, December 10, 1861, NBWM.

CHAPTER 9: THE CASE AGAINST CAPTAIN DAVOLL

1. *WSL*, July 11, 1862.

2. Ron Soodalter, *Hanging Captain Gordon* (New York: Washington Square Press, 2006), 150–51.

3. Abraham Lincoln letter, February 4, 1862, "Lincoln on the Execution of a Slave Trader, 1862," Gilder Lehrman Institute, www.gilder lehrman.org.

4. The court records are *John C. Warren qui tam v. Albert S. Bigelow, United States v. Edward S. Davoll et al.,* and *United States v. Pierre Pearce,* Federal Records Center, Waltham, MA. Columbo was not listed as a crew member, and the fact that he was from New York suggests that he might have had information about the *Brutus* during the time that Pearce attempted to fit out the ship there before transferring ownership to New Bedford.

5. *John C. Warren qui tam v. Albert S. Bigelow,* Federal Records Center, Waltham, MA.

6. Typhoid information is from the Reference Department, New Bedford Public Library.

CHAPTER 10: THE SHAM WHALERS OF NEW BEDFORD

1. Leonardo Marques, *The United States and the Transatlantic Slave Trade to the Americas, 1776–1867* (New Haven, CT: Yale University Press, 2016), 192–96; Kevin S. Reilly, "Slavers in Disguise: American Whaling and the African Slave Trade, 1845–1862," *American Neptune* 53 (Summer 1993): 188. The associates of Abranches, Almeida & Co. had been active in the Portuguese slave trade with Brazil. When that trade was disrupted by the British in 1851, the agents focused their attention on the Cuban slave trade and began operating out of New York. David Eltis, *Economic Growth and the Ending of the Transatlantic Slave Trade* (New York: Oxford University Press, 1987), 157–58. As noted in chapter 6, Abranches had made a personal visit to New Bedford to calm speculation that the *Atlantic* was being prepared for a slaving voyage.

2. The largest whaler was the *Sea*, an 807-ton ship that was based in Warren, Rhode Island, for a single voyage to the North Pacific from 1851 to 1855. *WSL*, March 1, 1859; *Parliamentary Papers, House of Commons and Command*, 70:116–17; American Colonization Society, *The African Repository* (n.p.: Nabu Press, 2012), 36:377; Trans-Atlantic Slave Trade Database, www.slavevoyages.org, voyage 4315.

3. Commodore Charles Wise to the Secretary of the Admiralty, August 9, 1859, *Parliamentary Papers, House of Commons and Command*, 70:116–17.

4. Warren S. Howard, *American Slavers and the Federal Law* (Berkeley: University of California Press, 1963), 2, 238.

5. Commodore Wise to the Secretary of the Admiralty, August 9, 1859, *Parliamentary Papers, House of Commons and Command*, 70:116–17.

6. Oaksmith's involvement with Walker's filibustering expedition is covered in John J. TePaske, "Appleton Oaksmith, Filibustering Agent," *North Carolina Historical Review* 34, no. 4 (1958): 427–47.

7. Machado, along with his partner, Mary J. Watson, hid behind legitimate business with Africa in palm oil and ivory but found human cargo more lucrative. See Marques, *Transatlantic Slave Trade*, 196–97, 215–16.

8. Statement of Ambrose S. Landre, *US v. Ship* Margaret Scott, box 225, Federal Records Center, Waltham, MA. *Seine* ownership in *Ship Registers of New Bedford, Massachusetts* (Boston: National Archives Project, 1940), 2:511.

9. Landre's statement, *US v. Ship* Margaret Scott, Federal Records Center, Waltham, MA; Reilly, "Slavers in Disguise," 185.

10. Ibid.

11. *New York Times*, November 11, 1862.

12. Reilly, "Slavers in Disguise," 189.

13. Ibid., 187; *WSL*, December 3, 1861.

14. Ron Soodalter, *Hanging Captain Gordon* (New York: Washington Square Press, 2006), 142–43; *New York Times*, June 16, 1862.

15. Consul Francis Lousada to Earl Russell, December 2, 1861, *Accounts and Papers of the House of Commons* (1862), 61:172.

16. While usually a minor shareholder, Kelley was the agent for the voyages of the bark *Byron* in 1855 and the bark *Hope* in 1856. *Ship Registers of New Bedford, Massachusetts*, 2:109, 259.

17. *WSL*, September 19, 1854.

18. Anita Manning, "Keaupuni: A Hawaiian Sailor's Odyssey," *Hawaiian Journal of History* 47 (2013): 91–94; Richard Henry Dana Jr. to Attorney General James Speed, April 4, 1865, Zeno Kelley Pardon Case File, A562, *United States v. Zeno Kelley*, National Archives, College Park, MD. An excellent recent biography of Dana is Jeffrey L. Amestoy, *Slavish Shore: The Odyssey of Richard Henry Dana, Jr.* (Cambridge, MA: Harvard University Press, 2015).

19. Manning, "Keaupuni," 93; Howard, *American Slavers and the Federal Law*, 235; Zeno Kelley Pardon Case File, National Archives.

20. Dana to Attorney General Speed, April 11, 1865, Zeno Kelley Pardon Case, National Archives; Manning, "Keaupuni," 98.

21. Dana to Attorney General Henry Stanbery, October 25, 1866, *U.S. v. Zeno Kelley*, National Archives.

CHAPTER 11: SLAVE TRADERS AND ABOLITIONISTS

1. Between 1850 and 1866, more than thirty-six thousand slaves were taken from Africa by ships originating in North America. Data from the Trans-Atlantic Slave Trade Database, www.slavevoyages.org. Mayor Fernando Wood quoted in Edward Robb Ellis, *The Epic of New York City: A Narrative History* (New York: Basic Books, 2004), 285.

2. The D'Wolfs financed at least ninety-six slaving voyages between 1787 and 1807. Leonardo Marques, "Slave Trading in a New World," *Journal of the Early Republic* 32, no. 2 (2102): 234–60.

3. Anne Farrow, Joel Lang, and Jennifer Frank, *Complicity: How the North Promoted, Prolonged, and Profited from Slavery* (New York: Ballantine, 2006), 46–49; Bernard Bailyn, "Slavery and Population Growth in Colonial New England," in *Engines of Enterprise*, ed. Peter Temin (Cambridge, MA: Harvard University Press, 2000), 254–55. A thorough treatment of Rhode Island's involvement in the slave trade is

Jay Coughtry, *The Notorious Triangle* (Philadelphia: Temple University Press, 1981).

4. Daniel Ricketson, *History of New Bedford, Bristol County, Massachusetts* (New Bedford, 1858), 252.

5. Kathryn Grover, *The Fugitive's Gibraltar* (Amherst: University of Massachusetts Press, 2001), 287, 136; Earl F. Mulderink, *New Bedford's Civil War* (New York: Fordham University Press, 2014), 28; Frederick Douglass, *My Bondage and My Freedom* (n.p.: CreateSpace, 2017), 123.

6. Grover, *The Fugitive's Gibraltar*, 104, 32, 167; Marques, "Slave Trading in a New World," 258–60; Donna McDaniel and Vanessa Julye, *Fit for Freedom, Not for Friendship: Quakers, African Americans, and the Myth of Social Justice* (Philadelphia: Quaker Press, 2009).

7. Weston quoted in Grover, *The Fugitive's Gibraltar*, 281.

8. Grover, *The Fugitive's Gibraltar*; Douglass, *My Bondage and My Freedom*.

9. Peggi Medeiros, "The First Baptist Pastor at Forefront of New Bedford Fight against Slavery," *SouthCoast Today*, February 24, 2018.

10. McDaniel and Julye, *Fit for Freedom*, 80; Mulderink, *New Bedford's Civil War*, 44.

11. French quoted in Grover, *The Fugitive's Gibraltar*, 15; Dana quoted in Jeffrey Amestoy, *Slavish Shore: The Odyssey of Richard Henry Dana, Jr.* (Cambridge, MA: Harvard University Press, 2015), 99.

12. Dewey quoted in Grover, *The Fugitive's Gibraltar*, 283.

13. Garrison quoted in Manisha Sinha, *The Slave's Cause: A History of Abolition* (New Haven, CT: Yale University Press, 2016), 314.

14. J. Taylor Wood, "The Capture of a Slaver," *Atlantic Monthly* 86 (1900): 451–63.

15. Winthrop D. Jordan, *White over Black: American Attitudes toward the Negro, 1550–1812* (New York: W. W. Norton, 1968), 220–21; George M. Fredrickson, *The Black Image in the White Mind* (Hanover, NH: Wesleyan University Press, 1987), 73–75; quotes by Rev. Theodore S. Wright and Stephen Myers are in Sinha, *Slave's Cause*, 315; Ricketson quoted in Grover, *The Fugitive's Gibraltar*, 284.

16. Briton Cooper Busch, *Whaling Will Never Do for Me: The American Whaleman in the Nineteenth Century* (Lexington: University Press of Kentucky, 1994), 33–34. For a thorough examination of black mariners, see W. Jeffrey Bolster, *Black Jacks: African American Seamen in the Age of Sail* (Cambridge, MA: Harvard University Press, 1997).

17. *New York Times*, September 21, 1861. New Bedford was not unique in this regard. As the historian Kevin Reilly explains, "Public support for abolition of the slave trade was also weak in major port

cities. The growing population of landless laborers and middle-class merchants involved in maritime affairs was not part of the abolition movement. Within the shifting port communities of New York and New England whaling centers, slavers were able to circulate and operate with all the immunity that their lucrative offers could buy." Kevin S. Reilly, "Slavers in Disguise: American Whaling and the African Slave Trade, 1845–1862," *American Neptune* 53 (Summer 1993): 183.

18. Log of the schooner *Palmyra*, October 14, 1861, NBWM.

19. Evelyn Hu-Dehart, "Chinese Coolie Labor in Cuba in the Nineteenth Century: Free Labor of Neoslavery," *Contributions in Black Studies* 12 (1994), http://scholarworks.umass.edu/cibs/vol12/iss1/5.

20. Grover, *The Fugitive's Gibraltar,* 132.

21. William W. Crapo, *Centennial in New Bedford* (New Bedford, 1876), 43, 45.

22. *WSL,* February 9, 1858. Even with the sharp decline in the use of whale oil for lighting, New Bedford's whaling industry lasted into the 1920s, kept alive by the increase in demand for baleen (whale bone) for corset stays, buggy whips, umbrellas, and other products. Eric Jay Dolin, *Leviathan: The History of Whaling in America* (New York: W. W. Norton, 2007), 356.

23. Kenneth M. Stampp, *America in 1857: A Nation on the Brink* (New York: Oxford University Press, 1990), 219–26; *WSL,* February 14, 1860.

24. Alexander Starbuck, *History of the American Whale Fishery* (1878; reprint, Secaucus, NJ: Castle Books, 1989), 660; Dolin, *Leviathan,* 338–39; *WSL,* May 8, 1860.

25. Michael P. Dyer, "The River and the Rail: The Industrial Evolution of the Port of New Bedford," *Industrial Archaeology* 40, nos. 1–2 (2014): 72.

26. Warren Howard, accounting for all hazards, calculated an average return on investment of 56 percent. Warren S. Howard, *American Slavers and the Federal Law* (Berkeley: University of California Press, 1963), 236–37.

27. The U.S. Navy was instructed that its primary goal was to protect American sovereignty against British naval searches of American vessels rather than cooperate with the more effective British efforts at capturing slavers. Donald L. Canney, *Africa Squadron: The U.S. Navy and the Slave Trade, 1842–1861* (Washington, DC: Potomac Books, 2006), 19, 31.

28. Charles Rappleye, *Sons of Providence: The Brown Brothers, the Slave Trade, and the American Revolution* (New York: Simon & Schuster, 2007), 322.

29. Ron Soodalter, *Hanging Captain Gordon* (New York: Washington Square Press, 2006), 213, 216.

30. The editorial was reprinted in the *New Bedford Republican Standard*, September 6, 1860.

31. Soodalter, *Hanging Captain Gordon*, 172; Leonardo Marques, *The United States and the Transatlantic Slave Trade to the Americas, 1776–1867* (New Haven, CT: Yale University Press, 2016), 234.

32. Mulderink, *New Bedford's Civil War*, 233.

33. ESD to Elizabeth Davoll, May 26, 1851.

34. *Harper's New Monthly Magazine*, June 1860, 19; J. Ross Browne, *Etchings of a Whaling Cruise* (New York: Harper & Brothers, 1846), 504.

35. *New York Times*, May 18, 1860. The Republicans, like Lincoln, were officially moderate on slavery, with no intention to prohibit the constitutionally protected right to own human property. But they were adamantly against the slave trade and the extension of slavery into the western territories of the United States.

36. Caleb Smith quoted in Soodalter, *Hanging Captain Gordon*, 151.

37. *New York Times*, November 17, 1862.

38. Adam Hochschild, *King Leopold's Ghost* (Boston: Houghton Mifflin Harcourt, 1998), 28, 225–34. Hochschild's account makes for horrifying reading but is essential for understanding the effects of slavery and colonialism in Africa.

39. Marques, *Transatlantic Slave Trade*, 225; Kevin Bales, *Disposable People: New Slavery in the Global Economy* (Berkeley: University of California Press, 2012), 8.

CHAPTER 12: THE CURIOUS CASE OF THE SHIP *B*_____

1. *New Bedford Sunday Standard*, October 2, 1921. I would like to thank Lenora Robinson for finding this intriguing story in the archives of the Mattapoisett Historical Society and bringing it to my attention.

2. The Nye family was well known and respected in New Bedford as master mariners and whaling agents. Pemberton Nye, age fifty-one at the time of publication, was a partner in a maritime supply store in New Bedford. See Alanson Borden, *Our County and Its People: A Descriptive and Biographical History of Bristol County, Massachusetts* (Boston: Boston History, 1899), 158–59.

3. The black oarsmen were identified as Kroomen, West Africans who sometimes acted as middlemen in the slave trade.

4. Edward Manning, *Six Months on a Slaver* (New York: Harper & Brothers, 1879; Kindle ed., 2017).

CHAPTER 13: CAPTAIN EDWARD S. DAVOLL (1822-1863)

1. Hannah Arendt, *Eichmann in Jerusalem: A Report on the Banality of Evil* (New York: Penguin, 2006).

2. Unknown writer, describing an 1857 voyage on the whaler *Leonidas* (1909), ms. 79, series L, S-S-10, folder 2, NBWM.

CHAPTER 14: CONSEQUENCES

1. Carrie Davoll, "Description of Westport Village," n.d., Westport Historical Society.

2. Agard Collection, NBWM.

3. *Representative Men and Old Families of Southeastern Massachusetts* (Chicago: J. H. Beers, 1912), 3:1285-86; Agard Collection, NBWM.

4. Ted Maris-Wolf, "'Of Blood and Treasure': Recaptive Africans and the Politics of Slave Trade Suppression," *Journal of the Civil War Era* 4, no. 1 (2014): 53-83; U.S. Supreme Court case 69 U.S. 383 (1865).

5. Agard Collection, NBWM.

6. Consolidated list of all persons of Class I, subject to do military duty in the Ninth Congressional District (Massachusetts); *Palmer Journal*, June 22, 1861. Additional information was provided by Cliff McCarthy, archivist at the Stone House Museum, Belchertown, MA.

7. Kevin S. Reilly, "Slavers in Disguise," *American Neptune* 53 (Summer 1993): 187; Agard Collection, NBWM. Some of this information came from a newspaper clipping on Oaksmith tucked into a Harvard Library copy of *The Life and Writings of Major Jack Downing of Downingville*, a popular book written by Appleton Oaksmith's father, Seba Smith.

8. *WSL*, June 24, 1862; *United States v. Ambrose S. Landre*, Federal Records Center, Waltham, MA; Massachusetts state census, 1865; New Bedford city directories for 1867 and 1869; U.S. Census, 1870.

9. *New York Times*, June 28, 1863; Anita Manning, "Keaupuni: A Hawaiian Sailor's Odyssey," *Hawaiian Journal of History* 47 (2013): 99; *Margaret Scott* case, Federal Records Center, Waltham, MA; Massachusetts death records and state census for 1865.

10. Zeno Kelley Pardon Case Files, particularly Richard Henry Dana Jr. to Henry Stanberg, October 25, 1866, National Archives,

College Park, MD; Peggi Medeiros, "City's Whale Ships Took Part in Slave Trade," *SouthCoast Today,* August 29, 2002, www.southcoast today.com.

11. Ronald Chen, "Rum and Tobacco for Slaves," *New Bedford Standard-Times,* March 12, 1978.

12. Jeffrey L. Amestoy, *Slavish Shore: The Odyssey of Richard Henry Dana, Jr.* (Cambridge, MA: Harvard University Press, 2015). For Dana's work with the Hawaiian witness on the *Tahmaroo* case, see Manning, "Keaupuni."

13. *New York Times,* August 28, 1861.

14. Leonardo Marques, *The U.S. and the Transatlantic Slave Trade to the Americas, 1776–1867* (New Haven, CT: Yale University Press, 2016), 249, 223; Green-Wood Civil War biographies, www.green-wood.com.

15. The *New York Post,* reprinted in the *New Bedford Republican Standard,* September 5, 1861; *New York Times,* November 17, 1862. On women in the slave trade, see Maria Vann, "Sirens of the Sea: Female Slave Ship Owners of the Atlantic World, 1650–1870," *Coriolis* 5, no. 1 (2015).

16. Sources for this speculation on the fate of the *Brutus* include "Testimony of a Hand on Board the Ship Brutus," *Boston Journal,* August 21, 1861; Agard Collection, box 3, folder 7, "Ship Brutus," NBWM; *New Bedford Republican Standard,* August 9, 1861; and the National Maritime Digital Library, https://nmdl.org.

17. Jamie L. Jones, "The Navy's Stone Fleet," *New York Times,* January 26, 2012; Earl F. Mulderink, *New Bedford's Civil War* (New York: Fordham University Press, 2012), 139–42.

18. *New York Times,* November 17, 1862; David Brion Davis, *Inhuman Bondage* (New York: Oxford University Press, 2008), 117.

INDEX

Page numbers in italics refer to illustrations.

ANTHONY J. CONNORS's career began with four years in the U.S. Coast Guard, followed by a BA and MA in English from the University of Rhode Island. He then spent thirty years in the computer software field, mostly as manager of training, documentation, and support. During his last fifteen years of work, Connors went back to graduate school and earned an ALM in history from Harvard Extension School and a PhD in American history from Clark University. In 2006 he received an International Center for Jefferson Studies fellowship to study at Monticello. Since retirement in 2006, he has been an independent historian, adjunct instructor at Clark and Suffolk Universities, and writer. His publications include *Ingenious Machinists: Two Inventive Lives from the American Industrial Revolution* (SUNY Press, 2014) and "Andrew Craigie: Brief Life of a Patriot and Scoundrel," *Harvard Magazine*, 114, no. 2 (2011). Connors lives with his wife, Sharon, in Westport, Massachusetts.

Printed in the USA
CPSIA information can be obtained
at www.ICGtesting.com
CBHW021217110724
11452CB00009B/199